G   ISSUES
IN A CHANGING WORLD

This new series of short, accessible think pieces deals with leading global issues of relevance to humanity today. Intended for the enquiring reader and social activists in the North and the South, as well as students, the books explain what is at stake and question conventional ideas and policies. Drawn from many different parts of the world, the series' authors pay particular attention to the needs and interests of ordinary people, whether living in the rich industrial or the developing countries. They all share a common objective: to help stimulate new thinking and social action in the opening years of the new century.

Global Issues in a Changing World is a joint initiative by Zed Books in collaboration with a number of partner publishers and non-governmental organizations around the world. By working together, we intend to maximise the relevance and availability of the books published in the series.

PARTICIPATING NGOs

Both ENDS, Amsterdam
Catholic Institute for International Relations, London
Corner House, Sturminster Newton
Council on International and Public Affairs, New York
Dag Hammarskjöld Foundation, Uppsala
Development GAP, Washington DC

Focus on the Global South, Bangkok
Inter Pares, Ottawa
Third World Network, Penang
Third World Network–Africa, Accra
World Development Movement, London

About this Series

'Communities in the South are facing great difficulties in coping
with global trends. I hope this brave new series will throw
much-needed light on the issues ahead and
help us choose the right options.'
Martin Khor, Director, Third World Network

'There is no more important campaign than our struggle to bring
the global economy under democratic control. But the issues are
fearsomely complex. This Global Issues series is a valuable
resource for the committed campaigner and the educated citizen.'
**Barry Coates, Director,
World Development Movement (WDM)**

'Zed Books has long provided an inspiring list about the issues that
touch and change people's lives. The *Global Issues for a New
Century* is another dimension of Zed's fine record, allowing access
to a range of subjects and authors that, to my knowledge, very few
publishers have tried. I strongly recommend these new, powerful
titles and this exciting series.'
John Pilger, author

'We are all part of a generation that actually has the means to
eliminate extreme poverty world-wide. Our task is to harness the
forces of globalization for the benefit of working people, their
families and their communities – that is our collective duty.
The Global Issues series makes a powerful contribution
to the global campaign for justice, sustainable and
equitable development, and peaceful progress.'
Glenys Kinnock, MEP

Critical Acclaim for this Book

'A concise, down-to-earth account of various pitfalls in the globalization process. It is essential reading for policy makers and negotiators, especially of developing countries.'
Yilmaz Akyüz, Chief Economist, United Nations Conference on Trade and Development (UNCTAD)

'A valuable contribution to the debate on globalization. It examines the implications of globalization for development from the perspective of the South. The simple exposition also makes it accessible to students, policy makers and concerned citizens.'
Deepak Nayyar, Vice-Chancellor, University of Delhi, India

About the Author

Martin Khor is the Director of Third World Network. TWN is one of a number of non-governmental organizations in different parts of the developing world which are concerned with understanding and influencing global policy. In this capacity, he has acted as a strong advocate on behalf of citizens' groups in the Third World on a range of international issues, including sustainable development, biosafety and other environmental questions, and the impact of globalization on the development prospects of the South. He received his original training in economics at the University of Cambridge.

He is a board member of the Consumers' Association of Penang (CAP), the South Centre in Geneva, and the International Forum on Globalization. He is also a former Vice Chairman of the UN Commission on Human Rights Expert Group on the Right to Development. He travels widely on speaking and other engagements and is the author of several books and numerous papers, occasional publications and newspaper articles on trade, development and environmental matters.

A GLOBAL ISSUES TITLE

RETHINKING GLOBALIZATION

Critical Issues and Policy Choices

Martin Khor

Zed Books
London and New York

University Press Ltd
Dhaka

White Lotus Co. Ltd
Bangkok

Fernwood Publishing Ltd
Halifax, Nova Scotia

David Philip
Cape Town

Third World Network
Penang

Books for Change
Bangalore

Rethinking Globalization
was published in 2001 by

In Bangladesh: The University Press Ltd, Red Crescent Building,
114 Motijheel C/A, PO Box 2611, Dhaka 1000

In Burma, Cambodia, Laos, Thailand and Vietnam:
White Lotus Co. Ltd, GPO Box 1141, Bangkok 10501, Thailand

In Canada: Fernwood Publishing Ltd, PO Box 9409, Station A,
Halifax, Nova Scotia, Canada B3K 5S3

In India: Books for Change, 28 Castle Street, Ashok Naggar,
Bangalore, 560025, India

In Malaysia and Singapore:
Third World Network
228 Macalister Rd, Penang, 10400 Malaysia

In Southern Africa: David Philip Publishers (Pty Ltd),
208 Werdmuller Centre, Claremont 7735, South Africa

In the rest of the world:
Zed Books Ltd, 7 Cynthia Street, London N1 9JF, UK and
Room 400, 175 Fifth Avenue, New York, NY 10010, USA

Distributed in the USA exclusively by Palgrave,
a division of St Martin's Press, LLC,
175 Fifth Avenue, New York, NY 10010, USA

A catalogue record for this book is available from the British Library
US CIP data is available from the Library of Congress
Canadian CIP data is available from the National Library of Canada

ISBN 974 7534 754 Pb (South-East Asia)
ISBN 1 55266 059 1 Pb (Canada)
ISBN 0 86486 493 0 Pb (Southern Africa)
ISBN 1 84277 054 3 Hb (Zed Books)
ISBN 1 84277 055 1 Pb (Zed Books)

NOTE

This book was first published by the United Nations Conference on Trade and Development (UNCTAD) as *UNCTAD Discussion Paper* No. 147 (April 2000) and is reproduced here with the permission of UNCTAD.
The text was circulated at the South Summit, held in Havana, Cuba on 10–14 April 2000.

CONTENTS

INTRODUCTION

Globalization has become the defining process of the present age. While the opportunities and benefits of this process have been stressed by its proponents and supporters, recently there has been increasing disillusionment among many policy-makers in the South, analysts and academics, as well as the community of non-governmental organizations (NGOs) in both the South and the North. The failure of the Seattle Ministerial Conference of the World Trade Organization (WTO) in December 1999 is a signal of this disillusionment.

The reasons for the changing perception of and attitude towards globalization are many. Among the important factors are the lack of tangible benefits to most developing countries from opening their economies, despite the well-publicized claims of export and income gains; the economic losses and social dislocation that are being caused to many developing countries by rapid financial and trade liberalization; the growing inequalities of wealth and opportunities arising from globalization; and the perception that environmental, social and cultural problems have been made worse by the workings of the global free-market economy.

This book examines the nature of economic globalization,

some of its key aspects (financial, trade and investment liber-alization), and recent developments and the implications for the South. It also provides proposals and suggestions on what could be done to reduce the negative aspects of globalization, and in particular what the countries of the South can do at the national and international levels to reduce the risks involved in (and better manage) the interface between the national economy and the global economy. While globalization is facilitated and influenced by technological developments such as modern information and communications technology, this book argues that the process is mainly driven and enabled by policy choices at the global and national levels that in recent years have led to the rapid liberalization of finance, trade and investment. Although developing countries have been very much a part of this process of rapid integration, the decision-making processes in the making of these policy choices have in the main been dominated by governments of the developed countries and by international institutions that are mainly under their control or influence.

The latest round of financial crises, starting with what happened in East Asia in 1997, the widespread doubts over the appropriateness of the standard policy responses to the crisis by international financial institutions, and the failure of the WTO's Seattle meeting, have catalysed a serious rethinking of the orthodox policies and approach to globalization and liberalization.

The rethinking exercise, which was most recently given a platform at the tenth session of the United Nations Conference on Trade and Development (UNCTAD X) in Bangkok in February 2000, provides an opportunity for the

South to take a more active role in reviewing recent developments in the global economy, their impact on developing countries, and the role these countries can play in reversing the negative aspects, while taking positive measures individually and collectively in pursuing more appropriate policy options and negotiating strategies (UNCTAD, 2000).

This book is organized into five chapters, following a brief introduction. Chapter 1 summarizes the main features of globalization, including economic liberalization, the globalization of policy-making, and the unbalanced nature and effects of the process. The next three chapters then examine the major aspects of economic globalization. Chapter 2 discusses trade liberalization, some recent findings on its effects, and recent developments in the WTO. Chapter 3 discusses financial liberalization, including the recent round of financial crises, the risks of volatile short-term capital flows, and deficiencies in the present financial system. Chapter 4 discusses investment liberalization, the nature of foreign direct investment (FDI) and the implications of the proposals and moves for international agreements on investment. In Chapters 2, 3 and 4, lessons to be learnt from the experiences of liberalization and proposals for improving the situation are provided. Finally, Chapter 5 draws some general conclusions and provides some general proposals.

CHAPTER 1

THE GLOBALIZATION PROCESS

The liberalization of trade,
finance and investment

Economic globalization is not a new process, for over the past five centuries firms in the economically advanced countries have increasingly extended their outreach through trade and production activities (intensified in the colonial period) to territories all over the world. However, in the past two to three decades, economic globalization has accelerated as a result of various factors such as technological developments, but especially the policies of liberalization that have swept across the world.

The most important aspects of economic globalization are the breaking down of national economic barriers; the international spread of trade, financial and production activities, and the growing power of transnational corporations and international financial institutions in these processes. While economic globalization is a very uneven process, with increased trade and investment being focused in a few countries, almost all countries are greatly affected by this process. For example, a low-income country may account for only a minuscule part of world trade, but changes in demand for or prices of its export commodities or a policy of rapidly reducing its import duties can have a major economic and social effect on that country. That country may have a marginal role in world trade, but world trade has a major effect on it, perhaps a far larger effect than it has on some of the developed economies.

The external liberalization of national economies involves breaking down national barriers to economic activities, resulting in greater openness and integration of countries in the world markets. In most countries, national barriers are being removed in the areas of finance and financial markets, trade and direct foreign investment.

Of the three aspects of liberalization (finance, trade and investment), the process of financial liberalization has been the most pronounced. There has been progressive and extensive liberalization of controls on financial flows and markets. The demise of the Bretton Woods system in 1972–1973 opened up an international trade in foreign exchange that has expanded at spectacular rates. The volume traded in the world foreign exchange market grew from a daily average of $15 billion in 1973 to over $900 billion in 1992 and now far exceeds $1,000 billion. Much of these transactions are speculative in nature, as it is estimated that only a small portion (less than 2 per cent) of the foreign exchange traded is used for trade payments.

Due to the interconnectedness of financial markets and systems and the vast amounts of financial flows, there is a general and increasing concern about the fragility and vulnerability of the system, and the risk of breakdown in some critical parts or in the general system itself, as a fault developing in one part of the world or in the system can have widespread repercussions.

The concerns about a possible global financial crisis have been heightened by the East Asian financial crisis that began in the second half of 1997 and which spread to Russia, Brazil and

other countries, causing the worst financial turmoil and economic recession in the post–World War II period.

Trade liberalization has also gradually increased, but not at
such a spectacular pace as with finance. World exports rose
from $61 billion in 1950 to $315 billion in 1970 and $3,447
billion in 1990. The share of world exports in world GDP
rose from about 6 per cent in 1950 to 12 per cent in 1973 and
16 per cent in 1992 (Nayyar, 1997). The increased role of
trade has been accompanied by the reduction in tariff barriers
generally in both developed and developing countries, due
partly to autonomous policies and partly to the series of multilateral trade rounds under the General Agreement on Tariffs
and Trade (GATT). However, high tariffs still persist in developed countries in sectors such as agriculture and textiles and
for selected manufactured products, which are areas in which
developing countries have a comparative advantage. Moreover, there has been an increased use of non–tariff barriers
which have affected the access of developing countries to the
markets of developed countries.

There has also been a steady growth in liberalization of
FDI, although again on a smaller scale than in the case of
international financial flows. Much of FDI and its increase is
due to flows among the advanced countries. However, since
the early 1990s, FDI flows to developing countries have risen
relatively, averaging 32 per cent of the total in 1991–1995
compared with 17 per cent in 1981–1990. This coincides
with the recent liberalization of foreign investment policies in
most developing countries. However, much of this FDI has
centred in only a few developing countries. Least developed
countries (LDCs) in particular are receiving only very small

FDI flows, despite having liberalized their policies. Thus, FDI is insignificant as a source of external finance to most developing countries, and is likely to remain so in the next several years.

A major feature of globalization is the growing concentration and monopolization of economic resources and power by transnational corporations and by global financial firms and funds. This process has been termed 'transnationalization', in which fewer and fewer transnational corporations are gaining a large and rapidly increasing proportion of world economic resources, production and market shares. Where a multinational company used to dominate the market of a single product, a big transnational company now typically produces or trades in an increasing multitude of products, services and sectors. Through mergers and acquisitions, fewer and fewer of these TNCs now control a larger and larger share of the global market, whether in commodities, manufactures or services. The top 200 global corporations accounted for $3,046 billion of sales in 1982, equivalent to 24 per cent of world GDP ($12,600 billion) that year. By 1992, their sales had reached $5,862 billion, and their equivalent value to world GDP ($21,900 billion) had risen to 26.8 per cent (Clairmont, 1996: 39).

The globalization of policy-making

Perhaps the most important and unique feature of the current globalization process is the 'globalization' of national policies and policy-making mechanisms. National policies (including in economic, social, cultural and technological areas) that until recently were under the jurisdiction of States and people within a country have increasingly come under the influence of international agencies and processes or of big private corporations and economic/financial players. This has led to the erosion of national sovereignty and narrowed the ability of governments and people to make choices from options in economic, social and cultural policies.

Most developing countries have seen their independent policy-making capacity eroded and have to adopt policies made by other entities, which may on balance be detrimental to the countries concerned. The developed countries, where the major economic players reside and which also control the processes and policies of international economic agencies, are better able to maintain control over their own national policies as well as determine the policies and practices of international institutions and the global system. However, it is also true that the large corporations have taken over a large part of decision-making even in the developed countries, at the expense of the power of the State or political and social leaders.

Part of the erosion of national policy-making capacity is due to the liberalization of markets and developments in technology. For example, the free flow of capital, the large sums involved, and the unchecked power of big players and speculators, have made it difficult for countries to control the level of their currency and the flows of money in and out of the country. Transnational companies and financial institutions control such huge resources, more than what many (or most) governments are able to marshal, that they are thus able to have great policy influence in many countries. Certain technological developments make it difficult or virtually

impossible to formulate policy. For example, the establishment of satellite TV and the availability of small receivers, and
the spread of the use of electronic mail and the Internet make
it difficult for governments to determine cultural or communications policy, or to control the spread of information and
cultural products.

However, an even more important aspect is the recent
process by which global institutions have become major
makers of an increasingly wide range of policies that were tra-
ditionally under the jurisdiction of national governments.
Governments now have to implement policies that are in line
with the decisions and rules of these international institutions.
The key institutions concerned are the World Bank, the
International Monetary Fund (IMF) and the WTO.

There are also other influential international organizations,
in particular the United Nations and its agencies, treaties and
conventions and world conferences. However, in recent
years, the UN has lost a lot of its policy and operational
influence in economic and social matters, and correspond-
ly the powers and authority of the World Bank, IMF and
GATT/WTO have expanded.

The Bretton Woods institutions (World Bank and IMF)
wield tremendous authority in a majority of developing
countries (and countries in transition) that depend on their
loans. In particular, countries requiring debt rescheduling
have to adopt structural adjustment programmes (SAPs) that
are mainly drawn up in the Washington institutions. SAPs
cover macroeconomic policies and have recently also covered
social policies and structural issues such as privatization, financial policy, corporate laws and governance. The mechanism

of making loan disbursement conditional on these policies has been the main instrument driving the policy moves in the indebted developing countries towards liberalization, privatization, deregulation and a withdrawal of the State from economic and social activities. Loan conditionalities have thus been the major mechanism for the global dissemination of the macroeconomic policy packages that are favoured by governments of the North.

The Uruguay Round negotiations greatly expanded the powers of the GATT system, and the agreements under the GATT's successor organization, the WTO, have established disciplines in new areas that go beyond the remit of the old GATT, including intellectual property rights, services, agriculture and trade-related investment measures. According to several analyses, the Agreement that emerged out of the Uruguay Round establishing the WTO has been an unequal treaty, and the WTO agreements and system (including the decision-making system) are weighted against the interests of the South. The existing agreements now require domestic legislation and policies of member States to be altered and brought into line with them.

Non-compliance can result in trade sanctions being taken against a country's exports through the dispute settlement system, thus giving the WTO a strong enforcement mechanism. Thus, national governments have to comply with the disciplines and obligations in the already wide range of issues under WTO purview. Many domestic economic policies of developing countries are therefore being made in the WTO negotiations, rather than in the parliament, bureaucracy or cabinet at the national level.

There are now attempts by Northern governments to expand the jurisdiction of the WTO to yet more areas, including rights to be granted to foreign investors, competition policy, government procurement practices, labour standards and environmental standards. The greater the range of issues to be taken up by the WTO, the more will the space for national policy-making (and development options) in developing countries be whittled away.

Another major development has been the proposal for a Multilateral Agreement on Investment (MAI). The attempts at an MAI in the Organization for Economic Cooperation and Development (OECD) have failed so far, while attempts have been made to begin negotiations at the WTO for an international investment agreement. The original MAI model would require signatory States to remove barriers to the entry and operations of foreign companies in almost all sectors, allow them full equity ownership, and treat foreign investors at least as well as local investors and companies. There would also be no controls over the inflow and outflow of funds, and requirements for technology transfer or other social goals would be prohibited. The MAI and similar types of investment agreements would be another major instrument in getting developing countries to open up their economies, in this case in the area of investment.

However, while the World Bank, IMF, WTO and OECD are the most powerful, the United Nations and its agencies also form an alternative set of global institutions. Recent years have seen several UN World Conferences on Environment (1992), Population (1994), Social Development (1995), Women (1995), Habitat (1996), Genetic Resources (1996) and Food (1996), and the UNCTAD Conferences (1996 and 2000). The UN General Assembly and its subsidiary bodies, its agencies, conferences and legally binding conventions, which are much more transparent and democratic, also influence the content of globalization as well as national policies, at least potentially.

The UN approach in economic and social issues is different from that of the WTO and Bretton Woods institutions. The latter promote the empowerment of the market, a minimal role for the State and rapid liberalization. Most UN agencies, on the other hand, operate under the belief that public intervention (internationally and nationally) is necessary to enable basic needs and human rights to be fulfilled and that the market alone cannot do the job and in many cases in fact hinders the job being done.

The Bretton Woods–WTO institutions have, however, become much more powerful than the UN, whose authority and influence in the social and economic areas have been depleted in recent years. As a result, the type of globalization promoted by the Bretton Woods institutions and WTO has predominated, while the type of globalization promoted by the UN has been sidelined. This reflects the nature of the globalization process. The former institutions promote the principles of liberalization and the *laissez-faire* market model and give high priority to commercial interests; thus they are given the role of leading the globalization of policy-making. The UN and its agencies represent the principles of partnership, where the richer countries are expected to contribute to the development of the poorer countries and where the rights of people to development and fulfilment of social needs are highlighted. The kind of globalization represented by the UN is not favoured by the powerful nations today, and thus the UN's influence has been curtailed.

Rising inequality and the effects of globalization

'Globalization' is a very uneven process, with unequal distribution of benefits and losses. This imbalance leads to polarization between the few countries and groups that gain, and the many countries and groups in society that lose out or are marginalized. Globalization, polarization, wealth concentration and marginalization are therefore linked through the same process. In this process, investment resources, growth and modern technology are focused in a few countries (mainly in North America, Europe, Japan and East Asian newly industrializing countries (NICs)). A majority of developing countries are excluded from the process, or are participating in it in marginal ways that are often detrimental to their interests; for example, import liberalization may harm their domestic producers and financial liberalization may cause instability.

Globalization is thus affecting different categories of countries differently. This process can broadly be categorized as follows: growth and expansion in the few leading or fully participating countries; moderate and fluctuating growth in some countries attempting to fit into the globalization/ liberalization framework; and marginalization or deterioration experienced by many countries unable to get out of acute problems such as low commodity prices and debt, unable to cope with problems of liberalization and unable to benefit from export opportunities.

The uneven and unequal nature of the present globalization process is manifested in the fast-growing gap between the world's rich and poor people and between developed and developing countries, and in the large differences among nations in the distribution of gains and losses.

The United Nations Development Programme's (UNDP) *Human Development Report 1992* estimated that the 20 per cent of the world's population in the developed countries receive 82.7 per cent of total world income, while the 20 per cent of people in the poorest countries receive only 1.4 per cent (UNDP, 1992). In 1989, the average income of the 20 per cent of people living in the richest countries was 60 times higher than that of the 20 per cent living in the poorest countries. This ratio had doubled from 30 times in 1950.

The *Human Development Report 1996* showed that over the past three decades, only 15 countries have enjoyed high growth, while 89 countries were worse off economically than they were 10 or more years earlier. In 70 developing countries, the present income levels were less than in the 1960s and 1970s. 'Economic gains have benefited greatly a few countries, at the expense of many,' said the report. Since 1980, 15 countries (mainly Asian) have had growth rates much higher than any seen during industrialization in the West. However, economic decline for most parts of the developing world has lasted far longer and gone deeper than during the Great Depression of the 1930s. While the rich countries mostly rebounded from the depression within four to five years, the 'lost decade' of the 1980s is in effect still continuing for hundreds of millions of people in many countries of Asia, Africa and Latin America. In some cases people are poorer than 30 years ago, with little hope of rapid improvement.

Wider inequalities among countries, as well as among income groups within countries, which are closely associated with globalization processes, have been examined in detail in UNCTAD's *Trade and Development Report, 1997 (TDR.97)*. It shows that since the early 1980s the world economy has been characterized by rising inequality, and North–South income gaps have continued to widen (UNCTAD, 1997: chaps. IV–VI). In 1965 the average per capita income of the Group of Seven (G7) leading industrial countries was 20 times that of the world's poorest seven countries; by 1995 it was 39 times as much. Polarization among countries has also been accompanied by increasing income inequality within countries. The income share of the richest 20 per cent has risen almost everywhere since the early 1980s while those at the bottom have failed to see real gains in living standards (in many countries the per capita income of the poorest 20 per cent now averages less than one-tenth that of the richest 20 per cent) and the share of the middle class has also fallen. The increasing inequality is noted in more and less successful developing countries alike, and in all regions, including East Asia, Latin America and Africa.

In the analysis of *TDR.97*, these trends are rooted in a set of forces unleashed by rapid liberalization that make for greater inequality by favouring certain income groups over others. They include the following: growing wage inequality in both the North and the South between skilled and unskilled workers (due mainly to declining industrial employment of unskilled workers and large absolute falls in their real wages); capital gaining in comparison with labour, with profit shares rising everywhere; the rise of a new *rentier* class due to financial liberalization and the rapid rise in debt (with government debt servicing in developing countries also distributing income from the poor to the rich); and the benefits of agricultural price liberalization being reaped mainly by traders rather than farmers.

There are some particularly disturbing aspects of the increased inequality. Firstly, the increased concentration of national income in the hands of a few has not been accompanied by higher investment and faster growth. 'It is this association of increased profits with stagnant investment, rising unemployment and reduced pay that is the real cause for concern' (UNCTAD, 1997: chap. VI). Secondly, some of the factors causing greater inequality in a globalizing world at the same time deter investment and slow down growth. For example: the fast pace of financial liberalization has delinked finance from international trade and investment; higher interest rates due to restrictive monetary policies have raised investment costs and led entrepreneurs to focus, instead, on buying and selling second-hand assets; the premium placed by global finance on liquidity and the speedy entry into and exit from financial markets for quick gains has undermined the 'animal spirits' needed for longer-term commitments to investment in new productive assets; while corporate restructuring, labour shedding and wage repression have increased job and income insecurity (UNCTAD, 1997: chap. VI).

Weaknesses of the South in facing the globalization challenge

Most countries of the South have been unable to reap benefits from globalization because of several weaknesses. Nayyar (1997) examines this phenomenon of 'uneven development', showing how globalization mainly benefits the developed world, while in the developing world, the benefits accrue only to a few developing countries. There were only 11 developing countries which were an integral part of globalization in the late 20th century. They accounted for 66 per cent of total exports from developing countries in 1992 (up from 30 per cent in the period 1970–1980); 66 per cent of annual FDI inflows to developing countries in 1981–1991; and most of portfolio investment flows to the developing world. Some of these 11 countries have since been badly affected by financial crises, debt and economic slowdown, thus diluting further the rate of success of the South in integration in the world economy.

The South's weaknesses stem from several factors. Developing countries were economically weak to begin with due to the lack of domestic economic capacity and weak social infrastructure following the colonial experience. They were made weaker by low export prices and significant terms-of-trade decline as well as the debt crisis and the burden of debt servicing. The policy conditionalities attached to loan rescheduling packages hampered the recovery of many countries and led to further deterioration in social services. Given the unequal capacities of North and South, the development of technology (especially information and communications technologies) further widened the gap. On top of these unfavourable international factors, many developing countries have also been characterized by dictatorships, abuse of power and economic mismanagement, which undermined the development process. All these factors meant that the South was in a weak position to take on the challenges of globalization, as the conditions for success in liberalization were not present. Given the lack of conducive conditions and preparedness, rapid liberalization caused more harm than benefit.

The South's weakness also stems from its lack of bargaining and negotiating strength in international relations. Being heavily indebted and dependent on bilateral aid donors and multilateral loan organizations, developing countries have been drained of their capacity to negotiate (even on the terms of loan conditionalities). The powers of the UN, in which the South is in a more favourable position, have been diminished, whereas the mandate and powers of the institutions under the control of developed countries (the IMF, World Bank and WTO) have been increased tremendously. The North has leverage in the Bretton Woods institutions and the WTO to shape the content of globalization to serve their needs and to formulate policies which the developing countries have to take on.

Although the North is in a dominant position and has been prepared to use this to further its control of the global economy, the South is also not helpless but can better organize its responses as well as its own proposals. However, the South as a whole has not done well in organizing itself to coordinate on substantial policy and negotiating positions, or on strategy in relation to the discussions and negotiations in the WTO and IMF as well as other forums.

The developed countries are well placed to determine the globalization agenda. They are well organized within their own countries, with well-staffed departments dealing with international trade and finance, and with university academics and private and quasi-government think-tanks helping to obtain information and map policies and strategies. They also have well-organized associations and lobbies associated with their corporations and financial institutions, which have great influence over the government departments. The developed countries also have institutions and mechanisms helping to coordinate their policies and positions, for example the European Commission, the OECD and the G7, and their subsidiary bodies and agencies.

In contrast, the developing countries are not well organized within their own countries. The government departments dealing with the interface with the global economy are understaffed, especially in relation to the rapid developments in globalization and in global negotiations. The academic sector and the few think-tanks which exist are not geared up to obtain and assess information on globalization trends, and less still to formulate policy proposals that governments can make use of. The links between these intellectual sectors, the NGOs and governments are also often weak. The business and financial community is not organized well enough to monitor global trends or to lobby governments on global issues. At the regional level, there is increasing collaboration among the countries through regional groupings. However, cooperation is still not as sophisticated as in the European Union. At the international level, the South is organized through the Group of 77 and the Non-Aligned Movement. These groupings often perform reasonably effectively within the UN framework and at UN meetings and conventions. However, they are not adequately staffed and are unable to keep track adequately of events and developments, or to formulate longer-term policies and strategies. At the WTO, IMF and World Bank, the collective strength of developing-country members has yet to be manifested in a strong way, although there are encouraging signs of more collaboration, for example at the WTO.

CHAPTER 2

KEY ISSUES
IN TRADE

Openness to international trade is not a recent phenomenon for developing countries. In the colonial period, they had related to the world market mainly as exporters of raw materials while importing manufactures. This division of labour is still prevalent for a large number of developing countries, whose exports comprise mainly a few commodities. Perhaps the most important aspect of globalization in trade for a majority of developing countries is the continuing decline in the terms of trade for their commodity exports *vis-à-vis* their imports of manufactures. The decline has become more acute in recent years, and has been responsible for the transfer of a huge volume of real resources from commodity-exporting developing countries through the mechanism of income losses arising from terms-of-trade changes. Other problems facing developing countries have been the pressures for import liberalization under loan conditionality; the imbalances in the Uruguay Round agreements; the lack of benefits relative to expectations accruing from the Uruguay Round; and the problems arising from their having to fulfil several of the WTO agreements. These issues are discussed below.

Commodity prices and terms of trade

The colonial pattern of trade, in which colonies exported raw materials and colonial master countries specialized in producing industrial products, has continued in the main to the present. Many Southern countries still mainly export primary commodities (mainly to the North) and import industrial products (mainly from the North). As the terms of trade of commodities have been falling continuously against manufactured goods, many Southern countries have suffered tremendous losses.

According to UN data, the terms of trade of non-fuel commodities *vis-à-vis* manufactures fell from 147 in 1980 to 100 in 1985 to 80 in 1990 and 71 in 1992. This sharp 52 per cent fall in the terms of trade between 1980 and 1992 had catastrophic effects. A paper by the secretariat of the United Nations Conference on Environment and Development (UNCED) in 1991 showed that for sub-Saharan Africa, a 28 per cent fall in the terms of trade between 1980 and 1989 led to an income loss of $16 billion in 1989 alone. In the four years 1986–1989, sub-Saharan Africa suffered a $56 billion income loss, or 15–16 per cent of GDP in 1987–1989. The UNCED study also showed that for 15 middle-income highly indebted countries, there was a combined terms-of-trade decline of 28 per cent between 1980 and 1989, causing an average of $45 billion loss per year in the 1986–1989 period, or 5–6 per cent of GDP (Khor, 1993).

In the 1990s, the general level of commodity prices fell even more in relation to manufactures, and many commodity-dependent developing countries have continued to suffer deteriorating terms of trade. According to the *Trade and Development Report, 1999* (*TDR.99*; UNCTAD, 1999a: 85), oil and non-oil primary commodity prices fell by 16.4 and 33.8 per cent respectively from the end of 1996 to February 1999, resulting in a cumulative terms-of-trade loss of more than 4.5 per cent of income during 1997–1998 for developing countries. 'Income losses were greater in the 1990s than in the 1980s not only because of larger terms-of-trade losses, but also because of the increased share of trade in GDP.' Moreover, the prices of some key manufactured products exported by developing countries have also declined. For example, the Republic of Korea experienced a 25 per cent fall in the terms of trade of its manufactured exports between 1995 and 1997 due to a glut in the world market (UNCTAD, 1999a: 87).

The income losses from falling terms of trade probably constitute the largest single mechanism by which real economic resources are transferred from South to North. These losses adversely affect the sustainable development prospects of the South as they contribute to the debt problem and to persistent poverty in many communities.

The world trading system has been favouring the exporters of manufactured goods, while proving to be disadvantageous to the many developing countries whose main participation in global trade has consisted in the export of raw materials and commodities and the import of finished products. Many Southern countries have lost their self-reliance in terms of producing their own food, as lands were converted to farm export crops that in many cases yielded unsatisfactory results in terms of instability of price and demand.

Attempts were made by developing countries to obtain fairer prices and more stable demand conditions for their commodities through commodity agreements involving producer and consumer countries, under the auspices of UNCTAD. Most of these agreements collapsed when the industrial countries, which are the main consumers of commodities, withdrew support in the 1980s. Many Southern countries, especially in Africa, are thus today subjected to an even greater extent to the vagaries of the commodity markets.

With oversupply of many commodities and stagnating demand and trend decline in prices, many developing countries still dependent on commodity exports have been trapped in a bad corner of the world trading system.

The commodities situation may worsen for developing countries should major consumer countries (in the North) develop laboratory substitutes for natural commodities through the use of biotechnology. There would be more displacement of the South's export commodities.

Proposals

(i)   The problem of trend decline in commodity prices and in the South's terms of trade should be seriously addressed through an international conference or convention, or other institutional mechanisms. It is imperative that such huge income losses incurred by poor countries be stemmed.

(ii) Countries could reconsider their attitude towards commodity agreements or other methods of cooperation between producers and consumers, since leaving commodity trade to the full force of highly concentrated markets has resulted in negative social and environmental effects. One possibility is to initiate a new round of commodity agreements aimed at rationalizing the supply of raw materials (to take into account the need to reduce depletion of non-renewable natural resources) while

ensuring fair and sufficiently high prices (to reflect ecological and social values of the resources).

(iii) In the absence of joint producer–consumer attempts to
improve the commodity situation, producers of export
commodities could take their own initiative to rationalize
their global supply so as to better match the profile of
global demand. The recent sharp increase in the price of
oil as a result of better coordination among producing
countries is a good reminder of the benefits that
producers can derive from greater cooperation.

(iv) An improvement of the South's terms of trade *vis-à-vis* the
North would be a valuable mechanism to stem and
reverse the current South-to-North flow of economic
resources. It would help create conditions for a more
equitable trading system, reduce resource wastage and
unsustainable consumption patterns, and expand financial
resources in the South for the transition to sustainable
development.

(v) The relevant international agencies including UNCTAD
should monitor and analyse the implications of biotechnology for developing-country commodities. Measures
should be taken if impact assessments show significant
negative effects on incomes and livelihoods in the South.
Signatory members of the Biosafety Protocol under the
UN Convention on Biological Diversity should exercise
the protocol's mandate to consider the social implications
of developments in biotechnology, especially for developing countries.

Trade liberalization

The benefits and costs of trade liberalization for developing countries constitute an increasingly controversial issue. The conventional view that trade liberalization is necessary and has automatic and generally positive effects for development is being challenged empirically and analytically. It is timely to examine the record and to formulate appropriate approaches towards trade policy in developing countries.

There is a paradox in the approach developing countries in general, and many scholars, take towards this issue. On the one hand, it is almost invariably repeated that 'we are committed to trade liberalization, which is positive for and essential to growth and development'. On the other hand, many developing countries also notice, and are now actively complaining, that trade liberalization has produced negative results for their economies or has marginalized them.

The notion that all are gainers and there are no losers in trade liberalization has proven to be overly simplistic. Some countries have gained more than others; and many (especially the poorest countries) have not gained at all but may well have suffered severe loss to their economic standing. Only a few countries have enjoyed moderate or high growth in the last two decades, while an astonishing number have actually suffered declines in living standards (measured in per capita income). The UNDP's *Human Development Report 1999* states: 'The top fifth of the world's people in the richest countries enjoy 82 per cent of the expanding export trade and 68 per cent of FDI – the bottom fifth, barely more than 1 per cent. These trends reinforce economic stagnation and low human development. Only 33 countries managed to sustain 3 per cent annual growth during 1980–1996. For 59 countries (mainly in sub-Saharan Africa and Eastern Europe and the CIS) GNP per capita declined. Economic integration is thus dividing developing and transition economies into those that are benefiting from global opportunities and those that are not' (UNDP, 1999: 31).

A clear explanation of why trade liberalization has had negative results is found in *TDR.99*. The report found that for developing countries (excluding China) the average trade deficit in the 1990s was higher than in the 1970s by 3 percentage points of GDP while the average growth rate was lower by 2 percentage points. In discussing why trade deficits have been increasing faster than income in developing countries, the report concludes: 'The evidence shows that a combination of declining terms of trade, slow growth in industrial countries and "big bang" liberalization of trade and of the capital account in developing countries has been a decisive factor' (UNCTAD, 1999a: chap. VI).

On the role of rapid trade liberalization in generating the wider trade deficits, the UNCTAD report said: 'It (trade liberalization) led to a sharp increase in their import propensity, but exports failed to keep pace, particularly where liberalization was a response to the failure to establish competitive industries behind high barriers. With the notable exception of China, liberalization has resulted in a general widening of the gap between the annual growth of imports and exports in the 1990s, but the impact was particularly severe in Latin America, where the gap averaged about 4 percentage points'.

One conclusion that can be drawn from the report is that if trade liberalization is carried out in an inappropriate manner in countries that are not ready or able to cope or which face conditions that are unfavourable, it can contribute to a vicious cycle of trade and balance-of-payments deficits, financial instability, debt and recession.

The UNCTAD report's findings correspond with some recent studies that show there is no automatic correlation between trade liberalization and growth. Countries that rapidly liberalized their imports did not necessarily grow faster than those that liberalized more gradually or in more strategic ways.

For example, in a study of 41 least developed countries, the UNCTAD senior researcher Mehdi Shafaeddin (1994) found 'no clear and systematic association since the early 1980s between trade liberalization and devaluation, on the one hand, and the growth and diversification of output and growth of output and exports of LDCs on the other. In fact, trade liberalization has been accompanied by deindustrialization in many LDCs, and where export expanded it was not always accompanied by the expansion of supply capacity'. By contrast, the paper attributes the success or failure of GDP and industrial growth to the volume of investment and availability of imports. 'The design of trade policy reforms has also been an important factor in performance failure.'

The Harvard University economist Dani Rodrik (1999) argues that developing nations must participate in the world economy on their own terms, not the terms 'dictated' by global markets and multilateral institutions. Noting the premise that reducing barriers to imports and opening to capital flows would increase growth and reduce poverty in developing countries, Rodrik's study concludes: 'The trouble is, there is no convincing evidence that openness, in the sense of low barriers to trade and capital flows, systematically produces these results. The lesson of history is that ultimately all successful countries develop their own brands of national capitalism. The States which have done best in the post-war period devised domestic investment plans to kick-start growth and established institutions of conflict management. An open trade regime, on its own, will not set an economy on a sustained growth path'.

A major problem faced by developing countries in the trade liberalization process is that a country may be able to control how fast to liberalize its imports (and thus increase the inflow of products) but cannot determine by itself how fast its exports grow. Export performance partly depends on the prices of the existing exported products (and developing countries have suffered from serious declines in the prices of their commodity exports and their terms of trade) and also on having or developing the infrastructure, human and enterprise capacity for new exports (which is a long-term process and not easily achieved).

Export performance in developing countries also depends on whether there is market access for the country's potential exports, especially in developed countries. Herein lies a major problem beyond the control of the South, for as is well known there are many tariff and non-tariff barriers in the North to the potential exports of developing countries. Unless these barriers are removed, the South's export potential will not be realized. As an UNCTAD note on *TDR.99* put it: 'Developing countries have been striving hard, often at considerable cost, to integrate more closely into the world economy. But protectionism in the developed countries has prevented them from fully exploiting their existing or potential competitive advantage. In low-technology industries alone, developing countries are missing out on an additional $700 billion in annual export earnings as a result of trade barriers. This represents at least four times the average annual private foreign capital inflows in the 1990s (including FDI)' (UNCTAD, 1999b).

Thus, trade liberalization can (and often does) cause imports to surge without a corresponding (or correspondingly large) surge in exports. This can cause the widening of trade deficits, deterioration in the balance of payments and the continuation or worsening of external debt, which act to constrain growth prospects and often result in persistent stagnation or recession.

Proposals

(i) Trade liberalization should not be pursued automatically, rapidly, as an end in itself, or in a 'big bang' manner. Rather, what is important is the quality, timing, sequencing and scope of liberalization (especially import liberalization), and how the process is accompanied by (or preceded by) other factors such as the strengthening of local enterprises and farms, human resource and technological development, as well as the build-up of export capacity and markets. A logical conclusion must be that if conditions for success are not present yet in a country, then to proceed with liberalization can lead to specific negative results or even a general situation of persistent recession. Thus, to pressurize such countries to liberalize would be to help lead them into an economic quagmire. Multilateral institutions should therefore not take the approach of putting pressure on developing countries to liberalize their trade rapidly.

(ii) Developing countries must have the ability, freedom and flexibility to make strategic choices in finance, trade and investment policies, where they can decide on the rate and scope of liberalization and combine this appropriately with the defence of local firms and farms.

(iii) Caution must thus be exercised when considering proposals for measures that would bind developing countries to further import liberalization, for example through proposed new issues (such as another round of industrial tariff cuts) in the WTO. Imbalances and inequities in the world trading system should be tackled as a priority; in doing so, developed countries should increase the access to their markets for products from developing countries, but they should not press the developing countries to further open up their markets to Northern products. Developing countries should be allowed greater flexibility to choose their own rate of trade liberalization.

The WTO and the multilateral trading system

The failure of the WTO's Ministerial meeting in Seattle in December 1999 presents an opportunity for all countries, especially developing countries, to review the framework, rules and effects of the multilateral trading system from the viewpoint of development and the interests of developing countries. The collapse of the Seattle meeting had its roots in both the system of decision-making and the substance of the negotiations. In the many months of the preparatory phase towards Seattle, developing countries generally were more concerned about their non-benefits from the WTO agreements and about the need to correct the problems of implementation of the agreements. Most of them were not in the frame of mind to consider or welcome the new issues being proposed by developed countries. The latter, on the other hand, were strongly promoting several new issues, such as investment, competition policy, transparency in government procurement, a new round of industrial tariff cuts, and labour and environmental standards. At Seattle, the United States' push for labour standards led by President Clinton (who linked the issue to the use of trade sanctions) seemed to confirm the fears of developing countries that the WTO was sought to be tilted even more against them by the major powers.

The clash of interests over substance was worsened by the organization of the meeting and the lack of transparency in the multitude of talks held in small groups that the majority of developing-country members had no access to. Many developing-country delegations made it clear, including through open statements and media conferences, that they would not join in a 'consensus' on any Declaration which they had little or no part in formulating. The talks had to be abandoned without the issuing of a Declaration by Ministers.

The tasks ahead in the needed reform of the multilateral

trading system include the need to address both substantive and procedural issues. The grievances of developing countries – that they have not benefited from the Uruguay Round and that the problems of implementation of the WTO agreements have to be rectified – must be urgently and seriously tackled. The process of decision-making and negotiation in the WTO has to be democratized and made transparent. 'Green Room' meetings that are not mandated by the general membership should be discontinued. Every member, however small, must have the right to know what negotiations are taking place and to take part in them. The following sections cover some of these issues in more detail.

Lack of realization of anticipated benefits for developing countries from the Uruguay Round

When the Uruguay Round was concluded and the WTO established, developing countries had expected to benefit significantly from increased access to the markets of developed countries for products (especially in the textiles and agriculture sectors) in which they had a comparative advantage. However, several years later, officials from many developing countries are complaining that their countries have not benefited and the expected benefits to them have not materialized due to the non-implementation of the commitments of the developed countries.

The main problems include the following:

TARIFF PEAKS REMAIN

A lowering of Northern countries' industrial tariffs is supposed to benefit those Southern countries with a manufacturing export capacity. However, 'tariff peaks' (or high import duties on certain products) remain in the rich countries for many industrial products that developing countries export. This means that some potential exports of developing countries are still blocked.

NO GAINS YET FROM THE SUPPOSED PHASING-OUT OF TEXTILES QUOTAS

The Uruguay Round's Agreement on Textiles and Clothing was aimed at phasing out the special treatment of the textiles and clothing sector, in which the developing countries for the past quarter-century had agreed to subsidize the North by allowing quotas to be placed on their exports in this sector. This 10-year phase-out was supposed to be the aspect of the Uruguay Round of most immediate benefit to the South, or at least the Southern countries that export textiles, clothing and footwear.

However, textile-exporting developing countries have been disappointed and frustrated that five years after the phase-out period began, they have not yet seen any benefits. This is due to the 'endloading' of the implementation of developed countries' commitments (that is, the liberalization with regard to most of the products they buy from developing countries will take place only in the final year or years), and the benefits will accrue only at the end of the 10-year phase-out period. Although developed countries have legally complied with the agreement by phasing out quotas proportionately, in fact they have chosen to liberalize on products that are listed but which they have not actually restrained in the past. As a result, developing countries have not benefited.

They have made proposals several times that the developed countries improve the quality of their implementation of the Agreement on Textiles and Clothing.

INCREASE IN NON-TARIFF BARRIERS SUCH AS ANTI-DUMPING MEASURES

Developing countries are also concerned that the supposed improvement of market access through tariff reductions is being offset by an increase in non-tariff barriers in the rich countries. A major problem has been the use (or rather misuse) of anti-dumping measures, especially by the United States and the European Union, on products of developing countries, including on textiles.

Many countries have proposed that the misuse of these measures be curbed by amendments to the Anti-Dumping Agreement.

CONTINUED HIGH PROTECTION IN AGRICULTURE

The Agriculture Agreement was supposed to result in import liberalization and reduction of domestic support and export subsidies for agricultural products, especially in the rich countries, and this was expected to improve the market access of those Southern countries that export agricultural products. As it turned out, however, the protection and subsidies have been allowed to remain very high. For example, in the initial year of the agreement, there were very high tariffs in the United States (sugar 244 per cent, peanuts 174 per cent); the EU (beef 213 per cent, wheat 168 per cent); Japan (wheat 353 per cent), and Canada (butter 360 per cent, eggs 236 per cent) (Das, 1998: 59). The rich countries have had to reduce such high rates by only 36 per cent on average to the end of 2000. The tariffs have thus still been very high, making it impossible for developing countries' exports to gain access.

Also, the agreement has allowed the developed countries to maintain most of the high subsidies that existed prior to the Uruguay Round conclusion. For example, they are obliged to reduce their very high domestic subsidies by only 20 per cent. In contrast, most developing countries had little or no domestic or export subsidies earlier. They are now barred by the Agriculture Agreement from having them or raising them in future (Das, 1998: 62). There is a great imbalance in this odd situation.

'Implementation problems' faced by developing countries from the Uruguay Round

Developing countries generally are also facing problems in their having to implement their obligations in the WTO agreements. The Uruguay Round resulted in several new legally binding agreements that require them to make changes to their domestic economic policies in such diverse areas as services, agriculture, intellectual property and investment measures. Many developing countries did not have the capacity to follow the negotiations, let alone participate actively, and did not fully understand what they committed themselves to. Some of the agreements have a grace period of five years before implementation, and this expired at the end of 1999. Thus, the problems arising from implementation may get more acute.

Main problems: The following are some of the major general problems:

- Having to liberalize their industrial, services and agriculture sectors may cause dislocation to the local sectors, firms and farms of many developing countries as these are generally small or medium-sized and unable to compete with bigger foreign companies or cheaper imports. This could threaten the jobs and livelihoods of local people.

- The Uruguay Round removed or severely curtailed the developing countries' space or ability to provide subsidies for local industries and to maintain some investment measures such as requiring that investors use a minimum level of local materials in their production. This could affect the viability of some local firms and sectors.

- The Agreement on Trade-Related Aspects of Intellectual Property Rights (TRIPS) will severely hinder or prevent local firms from absorbing some modern technologies over which other corporations (mainly foreign firms) have intellectual property rights (IPRs); this would curb the adoption of modern technology by domestic firms in developing countries. Also, the prices of medicines and other essential products are expected to rise significantly when the new IPR regime takes effect in the next few years.

The following is a summary of some of the concerns of developing countries regarding some of the agreements:

The Agriculture Agreement

The Agriculture Agreement could have severe negative effects on many Third World countries. Most of them (excepting the least developed countries) will have to reduce domestic subsidies to farmers and remove non-tariff controls on agricultural products, converting these to tariffs and then progressively reducing these tariffs. This will impose global competition on the domestic farm sector and may threaten the viability of small farms that are unable to compete with cheaper imports. Many millions of small Third World farmers could be affected. There is also a category of developing countries which are net food importers. As subsidies for food production are progressively reduced in the developed countries, the prices of their exports may increase; the net food importers may thus face rising food import bills.

A recent Food and Agriculture Organization (FAO) study of the experience of 16 developing countries in implementing the Uruguay Round Agriculture Agreement concluded that: 'A common reported concern was with a general trend towards the concentration of farms. In the virtual absence of safety nets, the process also marginalized small producers and added to unemployment and poverty. Similarly, most studies pointed to continued problems of adjustment. As an example, the rice and sugar sectors in Senegal were facing difficulties in coping with import competition despite the substantive devaluation in 1994' (FAO, 1999).

Proposal: Many developing countries, during the preparations for the WTO's Seattle Ministerial meeting, had proposed to amend the Agriculture Agreement to take into account their concerns on implementation, especially the effects on rural livelihoods and food security. Several developing countries have proposed that developing countries be given flexibility in implementing their obligations on the grounds of the need for food security, defence of rural livelihoods and poverty alleviation. They proposed that in developing countries, food produced for domestic consumption and the products of small farmers shall be exempted from the Agriculture Agreement's disciplines on import liberalization, domestic support and subsidies. This proposal should be pursued further by the developing countries in the future negotiations on agriculture at the WTO.

THE AGREEMENT ON TRADE-RELATED INVESTMENT MEASURES (TRIMs)

In the TRIMs Agreement, 'investment measures' such as the local-content requirement (obliging firms to use at least a specified minimal amount of local inputs) and foreign exchange balancing (limiting the import of inputs by firms to a certain percentage of their exports) will be prohibited for most developing countries from January 2000. Such measures had been introduced to protect a country's balance of payments, promote local firms and enable more linkages to the local economy. The prohibition of these investment measures will make the attainment of development goals much more difficult and cause developing countries to lose some important policy options to pursue their industrialization.

Proposal: Several developing countries proposed in the pre-Seattle negotiations in the WTO that the TRIMs Agreement be amended to provide developing countries the flexibility to continue using such investment measures to meet their development goals. In the review of the TRIMs Agreement, which was scheduled to begin in 1999, the problems of implementation for developing countries should be highlighted. The TRIMs Agreement could be amended to allow developing countries the right to have 'local-content' policy and to limit the import of inputs to a certain percentage of a firm's exports.

THE TRIPs AGREEMENT

The South's collective loss in the Uruguay Round was most acutely felt in the TRIPs Agreement, through which countries are obliged to introduce IPR legislation with standards of protection that are similar to those in Northern countries. This will hinder Southern countries' indigenous technological development. It should be noted that the present industrial countries did not have patent or IPR laws, or laws as strict as those that will now be imposed through the TRIPs Agreement, during their industrializing period, and this enabled them to incorporate technology originating from abroad in their local systems.

The agreement will also give rise to increasing technical payments such as royalties and licence fees to transnational companies that own most of the world's patents.

The new IPR regime will also have a significant impact on the prices of many products. By restricting competition, the IPR rules will enable some companies to raise the prices of their products far beyond cost and thus earn rents in terms of monopoly revenues and profits.

Also, most Third World countries have in the past exempted agriculture, medicines and other essential products and processes from their national patent laws, but with the passage of the TRIPs Agreement, all products are subject to

IPRs unless explicitly exempted. The prices of medicines are expected to shoot up in many countries, reducing access by consumers. The problem of the inability of AIDS patients in developing countries to have access to patented drugs due to their high prices has already become a major issue of concern. The TRIPs Agreement also opens the door to the patenting of life forms such as micro-organisms and modified genetic materials. Many environmentalists are concerned that this will be detrimental to the global environment as the present lack of controls and accountability in biotechnology research and application will likely accelerate biodiversity loss and could threaten natural ecosystems. For plant varieties, the TRIPs Agreement does permit countries the option to either introduce patents or institute an alternative 'effective' *sui generis* system of intellectual property protection. Many governments, NGOs and farmers' groups in developing countries are concerned that the practice of 'biopiracy' (patenting in the North of biological materials and resources originating in the South) will intensify. Moreover, unless appropriate *sui generis* systems are established in developing countries that protect the traditional knowledge and genetic resources of farmers, these farmers may be further disadvantaged by plant-variety protection regulations.

Proposal: Given these many problems, the TRIPs Agreement should be amended to take into account developmental, social and environmental concerns. Meanwhile, the grace period before implementation should be extended. Many developing countries made formal proposals before and at Seattle that a review of the TRIPs Agreement along these lines be made and that there should be an extension of the implementation deadline. These and other proposals can be pursued in the process of the review of the agreement.

Recently there have been calls from some eminent economists and from some NGOs to study whether the TRIPs Agreement should be taken out of the WTO. Their argument is that the agreement is a protectionist device and should have no place in an organization that is supposed to be committed to liberalization. Moreover, IPR is not a trade issue. By locating it in the trade system, the door is open to overloading the WTO with more non-trade issues.

CONCLUSION

These are only a few examples of serious problems facing developing countries in their implementing their WTO obligations, now and especially in future. Thus, many of the countries are arguing that they need time to digest the outcome of the Uruguay Round, and that some of the rules that are imbalanced or inequitable and that generate serious problems should be reviewed and amended. In fact some of the agreements themselves mandate that reviews be carried out. The next phase of the WTO's activities should focus on the review process, so that the opportunity to rectify the defects of the agreements can be taken. This review process would in itself be a massive task, involving analyses of the weaknesses of the various agreements, assessments of how they have affected or will affect developing countries, proposals to amend the agreements, and negotiations on these proposals.

Pressure for new issues in WTO

A major reason for the failure at Seattle was the reluctance of many developing countries to give the WTO a mandate for taking on new issues or negotiating new agreements, which had been proposed by some of the developed countries.

There is merit in the view that the WTO should focus in the next few years on reviewing problems of implementing the existing agreements and making the necessary changes in the agreements. These will be enormous tasks. They will not be properly carried out if there is a proliferation of new issues in a new round of negotiations. The extremely limited human, technical and financial resources of developing countries and their diplomats and policy-makers would be diverted away from the review process to defending their interests in the negotiations on new issues. The limited time of the WTO would also be mainly devoted to the new issues. Moreover, most of the proposed new issues would also have the most serious consequences for the South's future development. Issues such as investment rules, competition policy and government procurement are strictly not trade issues and it has been argued that they do not belong in the WTO. There is a suspicion on the part of some developing countries that these issues are sought to be placed there by the developed countries to take advantage of the enforcement capability (the dispute settlement system) of the WTO, so that disciplines can be effectively put on developing countries to open their economies to the goods, services and companies of the developed countries. Other issues relate to labour, social and environment standards. Most developing countries have argued that these issues should also not enter the WTO as they could be made use of as protectionist devices against the products and services of developing countries.

Should pressure continue to be applied for these new issues to be accepted into the WTO, then the WTO will continue to be split, and moreover, other pressing issues, such as the problems resulting from the existing agreements, will not be tackled.

General proposals

(i)   In the WTO, members should take a more realistic approach towards liberalization, and start to reduce the pressures being put on developing countries for further liberalization. If the developed countries continue after so many years to maintain such high protection in agriculture, textiles and some industrial products (and argue that they need more time to adjust), then developing countries should not be subjected to more pressures to continuously liberalize on the ground that it is automatically good for them.

(ii) It should be reasserted that the main objective of the multilateral trading system is the development of developing countries, which form the majority of the membership. Liberalization is a means, and there should be sufficient flexibility to implement measures when appropriate. The goal and dimension of development must be primary in WTO rules and in the assessment of proposals. The 'special and differential treatment' principle should be greatly strengthened operationally, above its present weak state.

(iii) Resolving the problems of implementation of the Uruguay Round agreements should be given top priority at the WTO. The following steps should be taken:

    (a) Developed countries should greatly increase access in their markets for developing countries' products, such as in agriculture, textiles and industrial products (where there are now high tariffs); moreover, they should stop taking protectionist measures such as anti-dumping measures;

    (b) In the areas where developing countries face problems in implementing their obligations, a systematic exercise to review and amend the existing rules should be carried out as a matter of priority;

    (c) In the meanwhile, where the transition period for implementation for developing countries has expired, an extension should be given at least until the review process is completed. There should also be a moratorium on bringing dispute cases against developing countries on issues where the reviews are taking place.

(iv) There should not be pressures to introduce new issues such as investment, competition, procurement, and labour and environmental standards in the WTO, as these would overload the multilateral trading system further and lead to more systemic stress and tensions.

(v) As the Seattle meeting showed, there is a need for serious reform of the system and culture of decision-making in the WTO. The reform process itself should be conducted in a manner whereby all members can fully participate. The reform should aim at a result whereby WTO meetings are run on the basis of full transparency and participation, where each member is given the right to be present and to make proposals. Even if some system of group representation is considered, all members should be allowed to be present at meetings and have participation rights. The WTO secretariat should also be impartial and seen to be impartial. The system should reflect the fact that the majority of members are now from developing countries, which have as great a stake or more in a truly fair and balanced multilateral system as the developed countries, and therefore the system must be able to provide the developing countries with adequate means with which to voice their interests and exercise their rights.

CHAPTER 3

KEY ISSUES IN FINANCE

Financial liberalization

Globalization in the financial sector has been driven by several factors. Among the major ones are: the policy choice of an increasing number of countries (starting with the developed economies, then taken on by many developing countries) of financial deregulation and liberalization (the opening-up by a country to international capital flows); the development of technology, especially electronic communications (facilitating massive cross-border movements of funds); the emergence of new financial instruments (such as derivatives) and financial institutions (such as highly-leveraged hedge funds); and the collapse of the international fixed exchange rate system (thus making it possible for profit to be made from speculation on changes in the rates of currencies).

Financial liberalization is a relatively recent phenomenon, but it has contributed to severe financial turmoil and economic losses in several developing countries that have integrated into the global financial markets. The developing countries had been drawn into the process of financial liberalization due partly to advice given by international financial institutions, and to the mainstream view that there were great benefits to be derived from opening up to inflows of international capital. However, the risks of also opening up to the volatility of short-term capital flows and to financial speculation and manipulation were not emphasized by the same advisors. Many developing countries that underwent the process of financial liberalization did not take precautionary measures or adhere to guidelines to minimize the risks. Instead, they went in the opposite direction by deregulating, removing existing capital controls, allowing private banks and companies to take foreign-currency loans, and allowing the trading abroad of their local currency.

Having deregulated and liberalized their capital accounts, many developing countries were unable to defend themselves from the huge flows of international funds whose volumes have expanded dramatically in the past two decades, and from the new financial instruments and institutions (especially highly-leveraged funds) that have emerged in the field of financial speculation.

Volatility and negative effects of short-term capital flows

The latest round of financial crises that hit emerging markets, starting with Thailand in mid-1997 and spreading rapidly to other East Asian countries before also affecting Russia and Brazil, has dramatically exposed the negative effects caused by volatile short-term capital flows and the grave risks and dangers that accompany financial liberalization in developing countries. The latest crisis has also exposed the fallacy of the orthodox view that opening up to global finance would bring only, or mainly, benefits, and little cost, to developing countries. The Asian crisis followed a period of financial liberalization, which contributed to a build-up of the countries' vulnerability to external financial forces. When large inflows of short-term capital took place, it led to an asset price bubble, which burst when speculative currency attacks and large capital outflows caused sharp currency depreciations which spread via contagion to other countries. The depreciations multiplied the burden of servicing foreign debt, which had been built up in a relatively short period, especially by the local companies and banks. When Indonesia, the Republic of Korea and Thailand ran out of foreign reserves to service the debts, they approached the IMF to bail them out with massive loans.

Almost alone among international agencies, UNCTAD had been warning for several years about the dangers and costs of financial liberalization. In the early and mid-1990s, its *Trade and Development Reports* and *Discussion Papers* had raised the alarm about the volatility of short-term capital and the serious destabilizing economic and social effects of financial liberalization, especially for developing countries. The Asian crisis validated the UNCTAD analysis and warnings. The crisis has also stimulated a general questioning of the orthodox approach and the start of a change in opinion and perhaps of paradigm.

As UNCTAD Secretary-General Rubens Ricupero stated, in his closing speech at UNCTAD X in February 2000: 'When trouble came, starting in Thailand in 1997, it brought with it a reversal of opinion. That episode revealed the sheer size of the financial flows that the industrial world could generate, relative to the normal size of flows of developing countries. The swift entry, and even swifter exit, of such massive flows made clear for all to see the havoc that can be unleashed on small and fragile financial systems that are open to such tidal waves of finance. Despite the commitment of many international agencies to the complete liberalization of capital markets right up to (and beyond) the hour of Asia's crisis, the same agencies now say that they can see some virtues in certain types of capital controls.... Positive processes of integration into the world economy are the goal. This has never changed. However, the liberalization measures that are necessary to this end must be phased in a prudent and orderly manner. They must take account of specific local circumstances, they must be complemented by appropriate domestic policies and accompanied by institution- and capacity-building. Only then can they hope to succeed' (Ricupero, 2000).

Also at UNCTAD X, Yilmaz Akyüz, Head of the UNCTAD Macroeconomic and Development Policies Branch, summed up the lessons of the crises that hit Asia and other regions as follows: 'The crisis has shown that when policies falter in managing integration and regulating capital flows, there is no limit to the damage that international finance can inflict on an economy. It is true that control and regulation over such flows may reduce some of the benefits of participating in global markets. However, until systemic instability and risks are adequately dealt with through global action the task of preventing such crises falls on governments in developing countries' (Akyüz, 2000).

One of the most incisive analyses of the Asian crisis is presented in the *Trade and Development Report, 1998* (*TDR.98*; UNCTAD, 1998: 53–109). It shows that financial crises are very much part of the global system and the Asian case is only one such. It gives a critique of how the IMF response converted a liquidity problem into a solvency crisis. Finally, it also proposes a range of crisis management measures, including a debt standstill and capital controls.

As *TDR.98* shows, the East Asian experience is only one in a series of many financial crises (for example, in the Southern Cone of Latin America in the late 1970s and early 1980s, Latin America in the 1980s, European countries in 1992, Mexico in 1994) over the past two decades. These crises are caused by the intrinsic and volatile nature of the global financial system after the closure of the fixed exchange rate system in the early 1970s.

Inappropriate response to debt crises and financial crises

A significant aspect of financial crises in developing countries is that the policy responses may often not be appropriate and could even make the situation worse. The 'structural adjustment' policies accompanying IMF-World Bank loans to heavily indebted developing countries as conditionality have been criticized for depressing their economies through high interest rates and large budgetary cuts; and many of the countries concerned have remained indebted.

The policy responses in the East Asian countries that also sought IMF assistance when the financial crisis broke in 1997 have also been widely acknowledged to be inappropriate. Once the countries fell into crisis, the IMF's response (monetary and fiscal tightening and high interest rates while maintaining or even extending capital mobility) made it worse.

In one of the deepest critiques of the IMF approach, *TDR.98* pointed out that the situation was characterized by a stock disequilibrium rather than a flow imbalance that could be corrected by expenditure reduction. The fall in the currency created a balance sheet disequilibrium for indebted banks, property companies and firms. The value of firms and assets thus declined. Since these assets had been the collateral for much of the increased lending, the quality of bank loans automatically deteriorated. Rather than ease the burden of refinancing on domestic firms by granting additional credit, the recommended policy response was to raise interest rates. This depressed asset prices further, and increased balance sheet losses of firms and their need to repay or hedge their foreign indebtedness quickly by liquidating assets and selling the domestic currency.

The report also pointed out that instead of the IMF loans going to support the new exchange rates, in East Asia the exchange rates were left to float. Thus, rather than guaranteeing the new exchange rate, the Fund's lending was aimed at ensuring the maintenance of the domestic currency's convertibility and free capital flows, and guaranteeing repayment to foreign lenders. The latter, unlike domestic lenders, emerged from the crisis without substantial loss, even though they had accepted exposure to risk just as other lenders had done.

According to UNCTAD, the crisis was initially one of liquidity rather than of solvency. As long as they were given sufficient time to realize their investments, the countries would have been able to generate foreign exchange to repay their external debt, with an exchange rate adjustment needed to restore competitiveness (which UNCTAD estimated at only 10–15 per cent, instead of the very sharp currency drops that took place). However, 'the use of high interest rates, the extent of currency devaluation and the reduction in growth rates that created conditions of debt deflation quickly acted on financial institutions and company balance sheets to create a solvency crisis'.

In other words, in this analysis, the crisis-stricken countries that sought IMF funds were never given a proper chance. What would that chance have looked like? According to *TDR.98*, given the sharp attacks on the currencies, the appropriate action would have been to move quickly to solve the problem by introducing a debt standstill and bringing the borrowers and lenders together to reschedule, even before the commitment of IMF funds. A combination of rapid debt restructuring and liquidity injection to support the currency and provide working capital for the economy would also have made it possible to pursue the kind of policies that enabled the United States to recover quickly from a situation of debt deflation and recession in the early 1990s. In the United States, in reaction to weakness in the financial system and the economy, short-term interest rates were reduced in the early 1990s to almost negative levels in real terms, thus providing relief not only for banks but also for firms and households, which were able to refinance debt at substantially lower interest-servicing costs. This eventually produced a boom in the securities market, thereby lowering long-term interest rates and helping to restore balance sheet positions, and thus providing a strong recovery. The policies pursued in the early 1990s were exemplary in the way they addressed debt deflation, making it possible for the US economy to enjoy one of the longest post-war recoveries.

UNCTAD's analysis thus shows the sharp contrast between the IMF's policy (which is influenced by the United States) of tight credit and high interest rates imposed on the affected Asian countries, and the United States' own policy of low interest rates and provision of liquidity.

In another interesting section, *TDR.98* (pp. 75–76) considers whether the Asian development model has been invalidated by the crisis. It notes the view of some Western commentators that blamed the crisis on the Asian countries' structural shortcomings (such as the close government-business relation and market distortions that insulated business from competitive forces and market discipline). However, while the East Asian economies are run differently from the Western model, the crisis does not differ from similar crises experienced by developed and developing countries, including those operating under the Western Anglo-American model.

The Asian crisis 'is yet another episode in a series of crises that have been occurring with increasing frequency since the breakdown of the Bretton Woods arrangements, and with the introduction of floating exchange rates and the unleashing of financial capital'. As in the earlier episodes of financial crisis and currency turmoil in developing countries, the East Asian crisis 'was preceded by financial liberalization and deregulation which, in some cases, constituted a major break with past practices. In this sense the fundamental problem was not that there was too much government intervention and control, but too little'. *TDR.98* draws the lesson that successful industrialization depends on how profits and integration into the global economy are managed. The Asian crisis confirms this: 'When policies falter in managing capital and integration, there is no limit to the damage that international finance can inflict on an economy'. There is certainly considerable scope for national policies in preventing and better managing crises of this sort, but 'these crises are a systemic problem, and action is therefore needed also at the global level' (UNCTAD, 1998: 76).

Lack of mechanisms for debtor–creditor burden-sharing

The latest bout of financial crises has again highlighted the absence of an international mechanism for the fair sharing of burden between creditor countries and debtor countries, and between international private creditors and domestic private debtors. In the absence of such a mechanism, unsatisfactory situations occur. In many cases, the creditors, being in a stronger position than a country facing default, can insist on full repayment, and with stringent terms of rescheduling of debt payments: for example, higher interest rates, or the government taking over (or guaranteeing) the debts of the country's private sector.

The creditors do not share fairly in the losses, while the debtor country has to assume all or most of the losses. This contrasts with a normal commercial situation, in which a credit-giving financial institution shares in the loss should the borrowing company get into difficulties or go into bankruptcy. Sometimes this kind of imbalanced 'solution' is mediated by international agencies. In other cases, the situation drags on, with the debtor country's government involved in prolonged bouts of negotiations with private creditor institutions without a clear solution, leaving the country in a situation of continuous debt. Only in exceptional cases is a heavily indebted country in a position to declare a default and take the lead in announcing measures implementing its intention only to partially pay back its loans to foreign creditors and investors.

The lack of a systematic and fair method of settling debts in conditions of financial crisis is a major disadvantage to developing countries, as they are usually the debtors.

Lack of transparency and regulation of international financial markets

The workings and movements of international financial markets have played the major role in financial crisis. There have been increasing calls from many quarters for reforms to these markets. Yet there is also a lack of transparency in what constitutes the financial markets, who the major players are, what moves and decisions they make, and to what effect. There are thus deficiencies in terms of the lack of transparency, information, monitoring and regulation of financial markets and the institutions that are major players in these markets.

Proposals

International-level proposals

GREATER TRANSPARENCY IN, AND REGULATION OF, INTERNATIONAL FINANCIAL MARKETS

There should be greater transparency in the way the financial markets operate. There should be more disclosure of the players and the deals in the various markets, including the trade in currencies. In particular, the funds available to, and the operations of, highly-leveraged institutions such as hedge funds, should be made public.

At the global level, there should be a system of monitoring short-term capital flows, tracing the activities of the major players and institutions, so that the sources and movements of speculative capital can be made known publicly.

There should be greater regulation of the behaviour and operations of financial institutions. A distinction should be made between legitimate forms of investment and speculation, and unethical methods of speculation and market manipulation. Regulatory measures should be taken to prevent, prohibit or control the latter.

There can also be serious pursuit of proposals for a global tax on short-term financial flows, such as the Tobin Tax, where a small tax (say, 0.25 per cent) is imposed on all cross-country currency transactions. This will penalize short-term speculators, while it will have only a very small effect on genuine traders and long-term investors. The advantage is that not only will speculation be discouraged, but there can also be greater transparency in the markets, as movements of capital can be more easily traced.

At the national level, in the North countries, which are the major sources of international capital flows and speculation, tighter national regulations can be introduced to curb excessive speculative activities. For example, banking regulations can be introduced to limit the amount and scope of credit to hedge funds.

DEBT STANDSTILL AND ORDERLY DEBT WORKOUT

Countries coming under speculative attack and which want to avoid an economic recession or collapse may have little choice but to resort to two presently unconventional measures – a 'debt standstill' (or temporary stop in servicing external loans), and capital controls. This is a conclusion in *TDR.98* on the management and prevention of financial crises. It reviews four lines of defence an indebted country can, theoretically, take if faced with a massive attack on its currency: domestic policies (especially monetary and interest rate policy) to restore market confidence and halt the run; maintaining sufficient foreign reserves and credit lines; use of an international lender–of–last–resort facility to obtain the liquidity needed; and a unilateral debt standstill, accompanied by foreign exchange restrictions and initiation of negotiations for an orderly debt workout.

Although the first three are theoretically possible, in reality they either do not work or are not in existence. Therefore, the fourth option should be considered seriously.

Under this fourth option (debt standstill and workout), *TDR.98* (UNCTAD, 1998: 89–93) has proposed the setting up of an international insolvency procedure whereby a country unable to service its foreign debts can declare a standstill on payment and be allowed time to work out a restructuring of its loans, while creditors would agree to this 'breathing space' instead of trying to enforce payment. This proposal is actually an extension of national bankruptcy procedures (similar to Chapter 11 of the United States Bankruptcy Code) at the international level for countries facing debt difficulties. Bankruptcy procedures are especially relevant to international debt crises resulting from liquidity problems as they are designed to address financial restructuring rather than liquidation. In an international system, one option is to set up an independent panel to determine if a country is justified in imposing exchange restrictions with the effect of debt standstills. The decision for standstill could be taken unilaterally by the debtor country, then submitted to the panel for approval within a period. This would avoid 'inciting a panic' and be similar to safeguard provisions in the WTO allowing countries to take emergency actions. These debt standstills should be combined with debtor-in-possession financing so the debtor country can replenish its reserves and get working capital. This would mean the IMF 'lending into arrears'. The IMF funds for such emergency lending would be much less than what is needed for bailout operations. The IMF can also help arrange for private-sector loans with seniority status.

As regards government debt to private creditors, reorganization can be carried out through negotiations with creditors, with the IMF continuing to play an important role in bringing all creditors to meet with the debtor government. For private sector debt, negotiations could be launched with private creditors immediately after the imposition of debt standstill.

The above proposal should be seriously pursued by developing countries. In the absence of such an international system, developing countries have been at the mercy of their foreign creditors and investors, who can suddenly pull out their funds in herd-like manner. Without protection, these countries first face a liquidity crisis which in turn produces a solvency crisis and then an economic crisis. If a Chapter 11 type of international bankruptcy procedure is in place, a country facing the imminent prospect of default can declare a debt standstill, get court clearance for protection from creditors, obtain fresh working capital, restructure its debts and plan for economic recovery, which in turn can eventually service the debts adequately.

With such procedures, countries facing a 'cashflow problem' can nip it in the bud and thus prevent a major crisis. Both the debtor country and its creditors gain. This would contrast with the present messy situation, where, in the absence of a fair system, all creditors rush to exit the country, each hoping to recoup its loan before other creditors take out theirs. When the debtor country has its back to the wall, the creditors as a group usually demand, in a restructuring plan, that the government not only pay higher interest on its loans but also take over or guarantee the payment of the loans contracted by private banks and firms.

INTERNATIONAL ENVIRONMENT ENABLING THE OPTION OF CAPITAL CONTROLS

The international orthodoxy of recent years, that developing countries would obtain great benefits while facing few risks in having a financially open system, is now losing credence in light of the extremely high costs being paid by several countries that opened up and experienced the sudden entry and exit of foreign funds, with the resulting instability and economic dislocation. A new paradigm is emerging that grants that developing countries should have, and indeed, should sometimes take, the option of maintaining or imposing capital controls to protect their interests and to enable a degree of financial stability. Especially in the absence of international regulation of capital flows, capital controls should not be taboo but be seen as a normal, acceptable and, indeed, valuable component of the array of policy options available to promote development.

This emerging paradigm is one of the outcomes of the recent round of financial crises. In order for developing countries to be able to exercise this option, however, the present prejudices against such controls should be removed. For example, the IMF has been advocating capital account convertibility as a key financial policy for developing countries and has been against their adoption of capital controls, even in times of financial stress and crisis. Since the IMF has a strong influence on developing countries, especially on those which are dependent on its loans, such a position constitutes a barrier to developing countries' ability to exercise the option. Therefore, there should be a change in the international policy environment or framework such that developing countries can adopt capital controls as part of their range of policies without their being looked upon with disapproval by international agencies or the developed countries. Just as importantly, moves or measures taken at the international level to pressurize developing countries towards rapid financial openness (for example, through adding capital account convertibility to the mandate of the IMF) should be reversed, if developing countries are to be able to choose the option of capital controls in a comfortable policy environment.

Capital controls are not a new measure but have, instead, been used by most countries until recently, and many nations still have them. *TDR.98* describes a wide range of capital controls that have been or can be used, and for which purposes. It concludes that in the light of the Asian crisis and the current international financial turbulence, to protect themselves against international financial instability, developing countries need to have capital controls, since these constitute a proven technique for dealing with volatile capital flows. Several other measures (such as more disclosure of information, better banking regulation and good corporate governance) that have been proposed by the industrial countries and the IMF have merit but are inadequate to deal with the present and future crises. Developing countries should thus be allowed to introduce capital controls, as these are 'an indispensable part of their armoury of measures for the purpose of protection against international financial instability'.

Controls on capital flows are imposed for two reasons: firstly, as part of macroeconomic management (to reinforce or substitute for monetary and fiscal measures), and, secondly, to attain long-term national development goals (such as ensuring residents' capital is locally invested or that certain types of activities are reserved for residents). Contrary to the belief that capital controls are rare, taboo or practised only by a few countries that are somehow 'anti-market', the reality is that these measures have been very widely used. In the early post-war years, capital controls for macroeconomic reasons were generally imposed on outflows of funds as part of policies dealing with balance-of-payments difficulties, and to avoid or reduce devaluations. Rich and poor countries alike also used controls on capital inflows for longer-term development reasons. When freer capital movements were allowed from the 1960s onwards, large capital inflows posed problems for rich countries such as Germany, Holland and Switzerland. They imposed controls such as limits on non-residents' purchase of local debt securities and on bank deposits of non-residents. More recently, some developing countries facing problems due to large capital inflows also resorted to capital controls.

Controls on inflows of FDI and portfolio equity investment may take the form of licensing, ceilings on foreign equity participation in local firms, official permission for international equity issues, and differential regulations applying to local and foreign firms regarding establishment and permissible operations. Controls on capital outflows can include controls over outward transactions for direct and portfolio equity investment by residents as well as foreigners.

Recent financial crises and frequent use of capital controls by countries to contain the effects of swings in capital flows point to the case for continuing to give governments the autonomy to control capital transactions. Ways have not yet been found to eliminate at the global level the cross-border transmission of financial shocks and crises due to global financial integration and capital movements. *TDR.98* thus concludes that, for the foreseeable future, countries must be allowed the flexibility to introduce capital control measures, instead of new obligations being imposed on these countries to further liberalize capital movements through them.

INTERNATIONAL MANAGEMENT OF EXCHANGE RATES

Since the end of the Bretton Woods fixed exchange rate system, currencies have been fluctuating to a lesser or greater degree. In recent years, it has become more and more obvious that the volatility of changes in exchange rates has become a major problem. Given the wild swings of exchange rates in some currencies, it is not tenable to hold that currency movements are only reflections of changes in the fundamental market values of these currencies. Instability of currency rates has become a major contributing factor to overall financial instability in affected countries and globally. As part of a reform of the international financial architecture, a more stable system of currency exchange rates needs to be established.

RESPONDING TO INTERNATIONAL PRESSURES FOR FURTHER FINANCIAL LIBERALIZATION

At least until the outbreak of the Asian crisis, there had been strong pressures emanating from international organizations for an international regime disciplining countries to open up their capital accounts, thus making freedom of the flow of funds (including those that are not directly related to trade or FDI) a standard and obligatory policy. For example, there have been moves to amend the Articles of the IMF to incorporate capital account convertibility as part of its mandate. In the proposed Multilateral Agreement on Investment that was negotiated within the OECD, one of the proposed clauses was on the freedom of foreign investors and funds to transfer short-term capital into and out of signatory countries. Although the two initiatives have slowed down (in the case of the IMF) or stalled (in the case of the OECD) at present, there could be a resumption of pressures to discipline developing countries increasingly to open their capital accounts. Such pressures should not be resumed, given the recent evidence of the possible negative effects of liberalizing the capital account on countries that were not yet prepared to withstand the potential shocks. While capital account liberalization may bring net benefits under some conditions, too little is yet known about the appropriate ways to manage the capital account, especially for developing countries. Thus, countries should be allowed to choose their own policies without facing pressures, either from international agencies or from other countries, to liberalize.

REFORM OF THE FRAMEWORK FOR MACROECONOMIC POLICY

The set of macroeconomic policies that forms a key part of the so-called 'Washington Consensus' (that puts the stress on 'getting prices right', withdrawal of the State from the economy and economic policy-making, heavy reliance on the free market, deregulation, privatization and liberalization, austerity budgets and high interest rates) has been at the centre of conditionalities attached to IMF and World Bank loans for indebted countries. These policies have come under heavy criticism, especially in the wake of the Asian crisis. The 'one-size-fits-all' approach towards economic reform and policy for countries in financial crisis should be changed to a more appropriate approach of seeking the right mix of policies to suit the particular conditions facing each country. Such conditions may vary from country to country, and thus the policy mix may also be different for different cases. Thus, the framework for macroeconomic policy advice or conditionality should be reformed to take into account these differences and in light of lessons to be learnt about which strategies have and have not worked in different circumstances. Countries must have the flexibility to choose from policy options, as it is not appropriate to present them with advice or conditions based on a single model or option.

National-level proposals

NEED FOR SERIOUS CAUTION ABOUT FINANCIAL LIBERALIZATION AND GLOBALIZATION

One of the major lessons of the Asian crisis is the critical importance for developing countries to manage properly the interface between global developments and national policies, especially in planning a nation's financial system and policy. While under certain conditions, liberalization can play and has played a positive role in development, the Asian crisis has shown up that in other circumstances, liberalization can wreak havoc. This is especially so in the field of financial liberalization, where the lifting of controls over capital flows can lead to such alarming results as a country accumulating a mountain of foreign debts within a few years, the sudden sharp depreciation of its currency, and a stampede of foreign-owned and local-owned funds out of the country in a few months.

It is therefore prudent for a developing country to take measures that reduce its exposure to the risks of globalization and thus place limits on its degree of financial liberalization. Countries should not open up and deregulate their external finances and foreign exchange operations so rapidly when they are unprepared for the risks and negative consequences. Measures should be adopted to prevent speculative inflows and outflows of funds, and to prevent opportunities for speculation on their currencies.

At the least, the process of opening up to capital flows should be done at a very gradual pace, in line with the growth of knowledge and local capacity regarding how to handle the new processes and the challenges that come with different aspects of liberalization. This will require policy-makers in all relevant departments to have a proper understanding of the processes at work, the policy instruments to deal with them, adequate regulatory, policy and legal frameworks, and enforcement capability. Moreover, the private sector players (including banks and other financial institutions, and private corporations) will also have to understand and master processes such as inflows of funds through loans and portfolio investment, the recycling of these to the right sectors and institutions for efficient use, and the handling of risks from changes in foreign currency rates.

The whole process of learning, training and putting the required infrastructure in place will need a long period. Some European countries, which started with already sophisticated financial systems, took more than a decade to prepare for liberalization, and yet failed to prevent financial disasters.

ESTABLISHING A COMPREHENSIVE NATIONAL POLICY TOWARDS
CAPITAL FLOWS

It is uncertain whether there will be any adequate reforms to the international financial system. Meanwhile, developing countries will still be subjected to volatile capital flows. It is thus imperative that developing countries establish a national policy framework to deal with international capital flows. In doing so, it would be useful to distinguish between the various types of foreign funds and their impact on recipient countries. Following this, measures should be considered to manage these different types of capital flows.

One of the critical aspects to look at is the potential effect of different types of funds on foreign exchange reserves and the balance of payments. This is because, in the present financially open system that most countries subscribe to, a country with inadequate foreign reserves or with a deteriorating balance of payments can begin to become seriously indebted, or be subjected to panic withdrawal of funds, speculative attacks and currency depreciation.

Foreign direct investment, portfolio investment, foreign loans and credit, and highly speculative funds are the major categories of foreign capital that flow in and out of a country. Since developing countries are too small to be big players on the global market, they can be very vulnerable not only to the decisions of the big institutions that determine the volume and timing of the flows, but also to the manipulative activities of some of the global speculative players.

However, developing countries can take some defensive measures, and must formulate a comprehensive policy to deal with the different kinds of capital flows. Such a framework may include: a selective policy towards attracting FDI of the right type; a careful policy on portfolio investment that welcomes serious long-term investors but discourages or prohibits the damaging short-term profit-seekers; a very prudent policy towards public and private foreign loans; and measures that as far as possible avoid manipulative activities and institutions.

Even with the best intentions and plans, there is no certainty that a country can be shielded from the adverse turbulent effects of global capital flows and financial operations. The national policies have to be augmented by international regulatory action, which is still absent. Until that comes about, if ever, each nation should look out for itself.

MANAGING EXTERNAL DEBT

External debt management should be accorded top priority in a nation's economic policy, as excessive debt can lead not only to a heavy burden on national resources but, even more seriously, to the loss of policy autonomy, and dependence on other countries or international institutions to formulate the nation's basic policies, and these externally made policies can be inappropriate and contribute to many years of economic and social deterioration.

Great care should be taken to limit the extent of a country's foreign debt to levels where it can be serviced with a margin of comfort. Developing countries should beware of the dangers of building up a large foreign debt (whether public or private), even if they have relatively large export earnings.

As the East Asian financial crisis showed, even countries that are big exporters, including of manufactured goods, should beware of believing that the export earnings would comfortably provide the cover for a rapid build-up of external debt. High export earnings alone are insufficient to guarantee that debts can be serviced. For a start, future export growth can slow down. There can also be a high growth in imports and a large outflow of funds due to repatriation of foreign-owned profits or due to the withdrawal of short-term speculative funds. In good years these factors can be offset by large inflows of foreign long-term investment. However, if the negative factors outweigh the inflows, the balance of payments will register a deficit, which contributes to the running-down of foreign reserves. If a point is reached when the reserves are not large enough to pay for current debt servicing, the country will have reached the brink of default and thus may have to declare a state of crisis requiring international assistance. In the affected Asian countries, their debt problems had been compounded greatly by the sharp depreciation of their currencies, thus raising equally sharply the burden of debt servicing in terms of each country's local currency and making the situation impossible to sustain.

Thus, having a large foreign debt puts a country in a situation of considerable risk, especially when the country has financially liberalized, has full capital mobility, and its currency is fully convertible and thus subject to speculation. A cautious policy should be adopted not only for public sector foreign debt but also for private sector bank and corporate debt. It would be a mistake to believe that if debt is contracted by the private sector, that would be safer than if the build-up is by the public sector. As the Asian crisis showed, private firms and banks can make mistakes, even bigger ones than governments, as much of the recent build-up of debt that became unrepayable was contracted by the private sector in Indonesia, the Republic of Korea and Thailand.

In particular, having too many short-term debts can be dangerous as they have to be repaid within a short period, thus requiring the country to have large enough reserves at that period to service these debts. The structure of debt maturity should be spread out, keeping in mind the dangers of 'bunching', or too much debt coming due at the same time. It is thus important to keep a watch on the relation of levels of debt and debt servicing not only to export earnings but also to the level of foreign reserves. Reserves should, if possible, be built up to a level comfortable enough for a country to service its foreign debt, especially short-term debt.

MANAGING FOREIGN RESERVES

The careful management of foreign reserves has thus emerged as a high-priority policy objective, especially in the wake of the recent financial crisis. Maintaining or increasing foreign reserves to an adequate level is a difficult and complex task. There are many factors involved, such as the movements in merchandise trade (exports and imports), the payment for trade services, the servicing of debt and repatriation of profits, the inflows and outflows of short-term funds, the level of FDI and the inflows of new foreign loans.

All these items are components of the balance of payments, whose 'bottom line' (or overall balance, either as surplus or as deficit) determines whether there is an increase or run-down of a country's foreign reserves. These items are in turn determined by factors such as the trends in merchandise trade, the external debt situation (in terms of loan servicing and new loans) and the 'confidence factor' (which affects the volatile movements of short-term capital as well as FDI). To these must now be added the state of the local currency, which (in the absence of capital controls) cannot be assumed to be stable; its level and movement have become major independent factors that both influence the other factors and are in turn influenced by them.

To guard and build up the foreign reserves, a country has

thus to take measures in the short and longer term to strengthen its balance of payments, in particular the two main aspects, the current account and the capital account. The first aspect is to ensure the current account (which measures movements of funds related to trade and services) is not running a high deficit. The second aspect is to build up conditions so that the capital account (which measures flows of long- and short-term capital not directly related to trade) is also manageable and well-behaved. These goals can be difficult to achieve especially in the present volatile circumstances.

NATIONAL CAPITAL CONTROLS

It was argued earlier that an international policy environment is needed that treats the use of capital controls as a normal part of national financial policy with the aims of shielding the country from the turbulence of potential volatile flows of funds and of having greater stability in the exchange rate. With a more sympathetic international environment, developing countries can then feel comfortable with using the option of selectively maintaining capital controls to regulate the inflow and outflow of funds. Some details of the use of capital controls have been given in the earlier section on international-level proposals. Further examples are given below.

To avoid excessive inflows or undesirable types of funds, various regulations can be introduced. For example, in Malaysia, there is a Central Bank ruling that, before taking foreign loans, private companies have to seek its permission, which will be given only if it can be shown that the projects can earn foreign exchange to finance debt servicing. Such a rule helped Malaysia to avoid building up the high levels of private foreign debt that had developed and led to the crisis in Indonesia, the Republic of Korea and Thailand. There can also be regulations limiting foreign portfolio investment and speculative behaviour in the stock exchange; that constrain currency speculation (for example, by limiting the amount of local currency loans to foreigners), and that prohibit international trade in the local currency. Regulations on capital outflows could include the prohibition of locals opening overseas bank accounts, limiting the types and amounts of transfers abroad, and constraining the overseas investments of local companies. The regulations can be varied or removed according to changing circumstances and developments.

Some of these measures were adopted recently in Malaysia as part of its response to the financial crisis. Another of its major measures was the fixing of the local currency to the US dollar. The package of measures is credited with helping the country to deal with the crisis and initiate a recovery process.

MANAGING THE EXCHANGE RATE

The management of the exchange rate to enable stability is one of the major challenges now facing developing countries. In a review of different systems of exchange rate management (from freely floating and pegged rates to currency board fixed-rate and dollarization systems), *TDR.99* has concluded that the key to having reasonable exchange rate stability is the regulation of destabilizing capital flows. Under free capital mobility, no regime of exchange rates will guarantee stable and competitive rates, nor will it combine steady growth with financial stability. 'Differences among systems of pegged, floating and fixed exchange rates lie not so much in the extent to which they can prevent volatility of capital flows or contain their damage to the real economy as in how the damage is inflicted. Damage can only be prevented or limited if there is effective regulation and control over destabilizing capital flows. While that may not be without cost, the cost is likely to be small compared to that of currency instability and mis-alignment and financial crises. Managing nominal exchange rates in a flexible manner in order to minimize fluctuations in the real exchange rate, in combination with controls on desta-bilizing capital flows, thus remains the most plausible option for most developing countries' (UNCTAD, 1999a: 130).

CHAPTER 4

KEY ISSUES IN INVESTMENT LIBERALIZATION

Introduction

Recent increased interest in the issue of investment liberalization and the desirability or otherwise of an international framework of investment policy and rules has been sparked by the proposal of the developed countries to introduce a legally binding international regime regarding foreign investment. This proposal emerged in a number of forums, especially at the OECD and the WTO.

Within the OECD, a Multilateral Agreement on Investment was the subject of intense negotiations by its member countries. It was the intention that OECD countries would first sign the MAI and then the treaty would be opened for accession to developing countries. However, the MAI negotiations have stopped, after protests by civil society and disagreement among the OECD members.

On a separate track, in the WTO, some developed countries in 1995 and 1996 also proposed negotiations towards a multilateral investment agreement (MIA). It was proposed that WTO general principles relating to trade (including reduction and removal of cross-border barriers, national treatment, most-favoured-nation treatment) as well as the integrated dispute settlement system (which enables retaliation and cross-sectoral retaliation) would now be applied also to investment. Many developing countries had objected to the issue of investment *per se* being brought onto the agenda of the

1996 Singapore WTO Ministerial Conference. However, discussion did take place in Singapore, and a decision was taken to establish a working group to examine the relation between trade and investment. This was meant to be only an educative process for an initial two-year period, and any decision to have negotiations for an agreement would have to be taken only on the basis of explicit consensus. In 1999, several developed countries led by the European Union were advocating that the investment issue be included in a proposed new round of multilateral trade negotiations to be launched at the Ministerial Conference in Seattle. However, several developing countries voiced the view that the 'study process' in the WTO working group should continue for some more years and that there should not be negotiations for an investment agreement, at least not at this stage. With the collapse of the Seattle meeting, there is at present no pro-gramme for negotiations for an investment agreement in the WTO, and the working group will presumably resume its study process.

A reading of the draft text of the MAI in the OECD and the European Commission's 1995 paper on 'A level playing field for FDI worldwide' shows that the MAI and the EC vision of an investment agreement in the WTO were basically similar in objectives and content. Both aimed at protecting and advancing the rights of international investors *vis-à-vis* host governments and countries. The main elements include the right of entry and establishment of foreign investors and investments; the right to full equity ownership; national treatment (treating foreign investors at least as well as local investors); the right to free transfer of funds and full profit repatriation; protection of property from expropriation; and other accompanying measures such as national treatment rights in privatization. A more recent EU paper at the WTO has proposed a more 'diluted' version of an investment agreement in the WTO, with a 'positive list' approach, in which members may list the sectors for liberalization and the extent of liberalization, and where the scope would be limited to FDI (unlike the OECD-MAI's broad scope that included all kinds of foreign capital). There is no doubt, however, that even the diluted proposal is aimed at increasing the pressure on developing countries to liberalize their foreign investment rules and to extend national treatment privileges to foreign investors. These pressures have increased the need for developing countries to examine the nature of foreign investment and review appropriate policies for managing foreign investment.

The benefits and risks of foreign investment

There has been a significant increase in foreign investment, including to developing countries, in recent years. Since the early 1990s, FDI flows to developing countries have risen relatively, averaging 32 per cent of the total in 1991–1995 compared with 17 per cent in 1981–1990. This coincides with the recent liberalization of foreign investment policies in most developing countries. However, again, there is a high concentration of these FDI flows to developing countries: much of the FDI is centred in only a few countries. LDCs in particular are receiving only very small FDI flows, despite having liberalized their policies. Thus, FDI is insignificant as a source of external finance to most developing countries, and is likely to remain so in the next several years.

The last few decades have also witnessed a significant shift of perspective in many developing countries towards foreign investment. In the 1960s and 1970s there was considerable reservation and mistrust on the part of the governments of many developing countries, as well as many development economists, towards foreign investment. Starting with the 1980s, however, there has been a growing tendency to view foreign investment more positively. A new orthodoxy came into being, that as a form of foreign capital, investments are superior to loans because investments (unlike loans) would not land the host country in a debt crisis. Indeed, foreign investment is being seen as a panacea for removing the obstacles to development.

Just as originally the view of many may have been extremely unfavourable to foreign investment, the pendulum could have swung to the other extreme to the extent that some now view foreign investment as an unalloyed blessing. In reality, there are both benefits and costs accompanying foreign investment. The task for policy-makers and analysts alike is to ascertain the determinants of the benefits and costs, and attempt to devise policies to increase the benefits and reduce the costs, with the aim of ensuring that there be net benefits.

This is especially so when little seems to be known of the effects of investment liberalization. At an OECD-organized workshop on FDI and the MAI in Hong Kong in March 1996, the keynote speaker, Dr. Stephen Guisinger of the University of Texas, said: 'Very little is known about repercussions of foreign direct investment liberalization on host economies...The link between investment liberalization and macroeconomic performance has received scant attention from researchers'.

Studies by the Malaysian economist Ghazali bin Atan (Ghazali, 1990; 1996) on the effects of FDI on savings, financial inflows and outflows, trade and growth conclude that successful growth in developing countries is premised essentially on raising the domestic savings rate to a high level and investing the savings productively. This is more important than the role of foreign capital, including FDI. The East Asian growth success is based mainly on high domestic savings rather than FDI. Foreign capital can help to supplement domestic savings but this has its downside.

There are three types of foreign capital inflow considered in Ghazali's studies: aid, debt and FDI. Foreign direct investment has many advantages (bringing in productive capital, foreign expertise, brand names, market linkages, aiding in industrialization, exports, employment).

However, there are also disadvantages or costs to FDI. These impacts need to be managed to ensure a net positive outcome. The study found that FDI has a negative effect on domestic savings, as it gives room for the recipient country to increase its consumption. FDI generates positive and negative effects on the flow of foreign exchange on two accounts: financial and trade. On the financial side, FDI brings in capital but also leads to a stream of outflows of profit and other investment income. This outflow increases through time as the stock of foreign capital rises. Thus, FDI has a tendency to lead to 'decapitalization'. Comparing aid, debt and FDI, the study finds that because of the much higher rate of return of

FDI compared to the rate of interest paid on aid or debt, the 'decapitalization' effect of FDI is greater than that of aid or debt.

On the trade side, FDI has a positive effect through higher export earnings and savings on imports (for products locally produced), but a negative effect through higher imports of intermediate and capital goods. It may also have a negative effect in raising imports of consumption goods. In many cases, FDI is heavily reliant on large imports of capital and intermediate goods. The high import content reduces the positive trade effect. Ghazali's study shows that generally there is a weak positive trade effect from FDI, although there is in some cases a negative trade effect. In order for FDI to have a positive effect on the balance of payments, there must be a strong enough positive trade effect to offset the negative decapitalization effect. However, due to the weak positive trade effect, or even a negative trade effect in some cases, there is a tendency for FDI to cause a negative overall effect on the balance of payments. Without careful policy planning, the negative effect could grow through time and become serious as profit outflow builds up.

Moreover, too rapid a build-up of FDI could lead to 'denationalization', where the foreign share of the nation's wealth stock increases relative to the local share. To avoid any economic or social problems that this may cause, Ghazali proposes that the rate of growth of domestic investment should exceed FDI growth.

Regarding the effect of FDI on economic growth, there are direct effects (which are generally positive) and indirect effects (which are generally negative, due mainly to the decapitalization effect). While the inflow of new FDI exerts a positive effect, the outflow of investment income arising from the accumulated foreign capital stock exerts a negative effect.

Given the various ways in which FDI affects the host economy, Ghazali (1996: 8–9) proposes that for FDI to be used successfully (with net overall benefit), the following conditions should be met:

(i) Availability of foreign capital does not detract from own savings effort;

(ii) The factor payment cost must be minimized and prudently managed;

(iii) Encourage or require joint ventures so that part of the return accrues to locals and is retained by the local economy;

(iv) Get foreign firms to list themselves on local bourses;

(v) To enhance positive trade effects, FDI must be concentrated in the tradeable sector, especially in export-based activities;

(vi) Local content of output should be raised over time to improve the trade effect;

(vii) The growth of domestic investment should exceed FDI growth;

(viii) To avoid reliance on foreign capital, developing countries should increase their savings rate and maintain sound economic and political conditions.

Ghazali's conclusions are that: 'The above are among

preconditions for ensuring successful use of FDI. Countries using FDI without regard to the above conditions would do so at their own peril. Any moves designed to prevent host countries from instituting such policies, however they are couched, are moves designed to keep developing countries at the bottom of the global economic ladder ... With the correct policies, FDI can be of great help to host countries. Without the correct policies, however, the use of FDI can lead to severe problems especially with regard to the long-term viability of the recipient's balance of payments'.

Several other recent studies have come to similar conclusions on the benefits and costs of FDI and the need for a regulatory policy framework.

In a survey of the effects of FDI on development, *TDR.97* (pp. 91–98) and *TDR.99* (pp.115–123) differentiate between different types of FDI, discuss its potential for causing financial instability and assess its impact on the balance of payments. *TDR.99* estimates that mergers and acquisitions formed half to two-thirds of world FDI flows in the 1990s. For developing countries, excepting China, the recent FDI boom has consisted predominantly of M&A, its share of total FDI to developing countries being 72 per cent in 1988–1991. Thus, much of FDI to developing countries is not in the form of 'greenfield investment' which creates new productive assets, but consists of the purchase of existing assets, especially through privatization and in the services sector.

TDR.97 shows that contrary to its image of being a source of stable funding, FDI can also be a source of considerable financial instability. Even when FDI is governed by long-term considerations, aggregate FDI flows can respond rapidly to changes in short-term economic conditions. Retained earnings (or profit reinvestment) is a major form of FDI, and some of these are invested in financial assets rather than physical assets. Changes in the rate and volume of reinvestment can result in fluctuations and instability of FDI flows to a country. Moreover, as pointed out by a World Bank study, a foreign direct investor can borrow funds locally in order to export capital and thereby generate rapid capital outflows; thus, it need not be the case that FDI is more stable than other forms of capital inflow.

On FDI's balance-of-payments impact, *TDR.99* (like Ghazali) also distinguishes two types of effects: net transfers (this compares FDI inflows with associated payments abroad such as profits, royalties and licence fees) and the trade effect (comparing exports from FDI with imports associated with FDI). Examining three case studies, it finds that in Malaysia the activities of foreign firms had a negative impact on both net transfers and the trade balance in the 1980s and early 1990s. Similarly, in Thailand FDI had a negative net impact on the trade balance in the late 1980s and early 1990s on top of rising payments abroad for profits and royalties, and these features of FDI contributed to external imbalances that played an important role in the country's subsequent crisis. For Brazil, the UN Economic Commission for Latin America and the Caribbean (ECLAC) secretariat has warned that 'in the near future there will be a significant deterioration in the balance of payments of transnational corporations in the Brazilian economy'. This is due to a trend of increasing remittances, rising concentration of FDI in the non-tradeable sectors, and the exhaustion of privatization-linked FDI.

The report also notes a worrying trend: there is a decreased association between FDI and export growth in developing countries. It quotes the conclusion of the Bank for International Settlements that for South and East Asian countries, there was a significant weakening of the relation between FDI and export growth in the 1990s (as compared to the 1980s) and this was a factor contributing to the payments problems and the crisis in East Asia. UNCTAD's own data for a larger number of countries shows this weakening of the link between FDI and exports is widespread in the developing world. The same FDI inflows were associated with less rapid export growth in 1991–1996 than during 1985–1990. A major factor was the increasing concentration of FDI in services sectors, which do not yield much export earnings (UNCTAD, 1999a: 123).

In a study on FDI and development, the South Centre (1997) lists the possible benefits of FDI as technology transfer; increased production efficiency due to competition from multinationals; improvement in quality of production factors such as management (including in other firms); benefits to the balance of payments through inflow of investment funds; increases in exports; increases in savings and investments and hence faster growth of output and employment.

The acknowledged costs include the possible negative effects on the balance of payments due to increased imported inputs and profits remitted abroad; the high market power of multinationals, which can lead to non-competitive pricing and its resulting overall inefficiency in resource allocation; adverse impact on the competitive environment; and discouragement of development of technical know-how by local firms. If it fails to generate adequate linkages with the local economy, FDI will have fewer spillover beneficial effects and may on balance be harmful if the other negative features above exist. Other costs are transfer pricing (which diminishes host-government tax revenues); distortion of consumption patterns due to brand names of multinationals (with detrimental effects when costly foreign foods from FDI supplant local and more nutritious foods in the diet of the urban poor); and the net loss of jobs when capital-intensive FDI displaces labour-intensive local firms.

There are also environmental and natural-resource costs associated with FDI, and the risk of FDI in the media facilitating western cultural hegemony. Also, politico-strategic interests are at stake if FDI constitutes a large component of total investment and involves loss of local control over strategic sectors, infrastructure and natural resources; while decisions made abroad can impact on the local economy and society, and sometimes even the country's sovereignty may be at stake. These factors have to be taken into account in an overall net evaluation of the costs and benefits of FDI.

Although there are arguments in favour of FDI, the study concludes that an undiscerning policy towards FDI may cause serious economic difficulties, harming a country's development prospects in the long run. Not all FDI is conducive to development – some kinds may do more harm than good – and a policy to accept any and all FDI may harbour trouble for a country's future development prospects. To limit the risks and avoid undesirable effects, the study recommends that governments adopt a selective policy towards FDI by determining the composition of capital inflows and intervening to manage these inflows including FDI; a selective policy with respect to specific projects, e.g., confining FDI to priority sectors; and prudence with respect to total FDI flows and stock to avoid more financial fragility. It concludes: 'A global investment regime that took away a developing country's ability to select among FDI projects would hinder development and prejudice economic stability'.

Regulation of and policy options on FDI

The major issue in relation to the desirability of a global investment regime is not whether or not foreign investment is good or bad or whether it should be welcomed. It is whether or not national governments should retain powers to regulate FDI and have policy instruments and options over investment, including foreign investment. Most countries presently accept the importance of foreign investment and are trying their best to attract foreign investments. However, there is evidence that foreign investment can have both positive and negative effects, and a major objective of development policy is to maximize the positive aspects while minimizing the negative aspects, so that on balance there is a significant benefit.

Experience shows that for foreign investment to play a positive role, government must have the right and powers to regulate its entry, terms of conditions and operations.

Regulations on entry and establishment
Most developing countries now have policies that regulate the entry of foreign firms, and include various conditions and restrictions for foreign investors overall and on a sector-by-

sector basis. There are few developing countries (if any) that have now adopted a total right of entry policy. In some countries, foreign companies are not allowed to operate in certain sectors, for instance banking, insurance or telecommunications. In sectors where they are allowed, foreign companies have to apply for permission to establish themselves, and if approval is given it often comes with conditions.

An international investment regime that grants rights of establishment and national treatment to foreign investors would put pressure on developing countries to give up or phase out present policies regulating the entry and the conditions of participation of foreign investors.

Policies favouring local firms and domestic economy

Many developing countries also have policies that favour the growth of local companies. For instance, there may be tax breaks for a local company not available to foreign companies; local banks may be given greater scope of business than foreign banks; only local institutions may be eligible for research and development grants; and local firms may be given preference in government business or contracts.

Governments justify such policies and conditions on the grounds of sovereignty (that a country's population has to have control over at least a minimal but significant part of its own economy) or national development (that local firms need to be given advantages or preferential treatment at least for some time so that they can be in a position to compete with more powerful and better-endowed foreign companies).

Most developing countries would argue that during the colonial era, their economies were shaped to the advantage of foreign companies and financial institutions. Local people and enterprises were therefore at a disadvantage and now require a considerable length of time where special treatment is accorded to them, before they can compete on more balanced terms with the bigger foreign companies.

Measures to manage the balance of payments

As shown earlier, there is a general tendency for FDI to generate a net outflow of foreign exchange. Many developing countries have taken measures to try to ensure a more positive result from FDI in the balance of payments and the domestic economy. These measures may aim at:

(a) increasing the share of export earnings (and thus foreign exchange) in the output of FDI (for example, incentives or permission for higher equity ownership are given to firms that are more export-oriented in order to encourage export earnings);

(b) reducing the imports of capital and intermediate goods by foreign firms through encouraging the use of local products;

(c) reducing the amount of foreign profits through requirements that the foreign firm form a joint venture with local partners or allocate a part of the company's shares to locals, so that a portion of FDI profits accrues to locals; and

(d) requiring or encouraging a foreign firm to retain a significant part of its profits for reinvestment.

The objectives are to generate spin-offs for and linkages to the domestic economy and thus boost growth, and also to attempt to get FDI to have a more positive impact on the balance of payments by increasing the share of revenue and value-added that is retained in the economy.

Some of the traditional measures have already come under pressure from the WTO's TRIMs Agreement. Proposals for an investment agreement that prohibits a wide range of 'performance requirements' (including not only the above but also many new items) would make the situation even more difficult.

Critique of attempts at international investment agreements

The proposals for a multilateral investment agreement, either at the OECD or at the WTO, seek radically to broaden the scope of freedom of movement and operation of foreign investors and their investments, and to provide more rights for them. Such an agreement would severely narrow and restrict the rights and powers of States to regulate the entry, establishment and operations of foreign companies and their investments. It would make host developing countries far more susceptible to legal action by foreign investors and their home governments due to strict dispute settlement procedures. Such an agreement would have serious consequences for developing countries.

Firstly, it is unlikely that the claimed benefits of such an agreement will be realized by most developing countries. Its proponents claim that an investment agreement would lead to a greater flow of foreign investments to developing countries that join it, and that this in turn is an indispensable condition for their development as it would spur economic growth. The main assumption is that foreign investment and its free movement only generates benefits for the host country and does not result in costs, and that thus any increase will necessarily contribute to development. This assumption cannot be empirically supported.

Given these complex realities, it is obvious that foreign investment has to be prudently and well managed, so that the benefits are well brought out and the costs reduced, and that the former exceed the latter. As this will happen only under certain conditions, the policy-makers in the host developing countries need an array of policy instruments in an attempt to achieve net positive results. In the past, and presently, these instruments have included careful screening of investments and various conditions imposed on approved investments, a wide range of performance requirements (including on technology transfer, establishment of joint ventures and local content), and controls on capital inflows and outflows (especially on loans and short-term capital). It is precisely these policy instruments that the proposed investment agreement is aiming to dismantle and make illegal. This would deprive developing countries of the opportunity or even the possibility of ensuring net benefits from foreign investment, and it would more than tilt the balance so that foreign investment would probably result in costs outweighing the benefits in many cases.

But even if a country is willing to take the risks of increased and unregulated inflows, there is no guarantee (and in many cases no likelihood) that there will be an increase in foreign investment in the first place. The flow of foreign investment is determined by many factors, of which the treatment and protection of investment is only one, and usually not the most significant at that. Other factors are the opportunities for sales and profits, the size of the market, the general level of development of a country, the state of the infrastructure and quality of labour skills, political and social stability, the availability of natural resources to exploit, and the location of the country. A developing country that joins the investment agreement but does not possess some or most of the above qualities is likely not to experience an increase in foreign investment. Many countries that liberalized their foreign investment regimes under structural adjustment programmes have not seen a rise in foreign investment inflow.

Indeed, it is likely that the least developed countries would be at the greatest disadvantage. More advanced developing countries have more of the attractive qualities (profitable market, infrastructure, skilled labour). An LDC can offset its lack of attractiveness by offering better treatment, protection or incentives. But if most or all developing countries were to join a multilateral investment agreement, then the LDCs would lose this advantage.

An MAI-type investment agreement would also potentially cause the following effects on developing countries: significant loss of policy autonomy over investment matters; erosion of sovereignty (including over natural resources) and of local ownership and participation in the national economy; and negative effects on the national financial position (Khor, 1999).

An alternative approach

The initiatives towards MAI were not of course the first attempts at establishing an international framework on foreign investment. However, the approach taken by the MAI proponents is new in that it is an extreme and one-sided approach that greatly expands the rights of international investors, while not recognizing, and thus greatly reducing, the authority and rights of host governments and countries.

This one-sided approach on behalf of foreign investors' interests is in contrast to some earlier attempts within the UN system to set up an international framework on foreign investment that sought to balance the rights and obligations of foreign investors and host countries, as well as to balance the foreign investors' production activities with development, social and environmental goals.

On a general level, the most well-known of these has been the Draft UN Code of Conduct on Transnational Corporations, which underwent a decade of negotiations from 1982 to the early 1990s under the UN Commission on Transnational Corporations, serviced by the UN Centre on Transnational Corporations (UNCTC, 1990).

The Code was an attempt at balancing the rights of host countries with the rights of foreign investors, and the obligations of TNCs with the obligations of host countries. The Code was also inclusive of many issues, including political dimensions (respect for national sovereignty, non-interference and human rights), development dimensions (transfer pricing, balance of payments, technology transfer) and social dimensions (socio-cultural values, consumer and environmental protection). The Code was placed in the context of international cooperation, recognized both the contributions and negative effects of TNCs, and sought to maximize the former and minimize the latter, towards the goal of development and growth. This is a more balanced approach than that taken by the MAI, which implicitly only makes claims for the benefits of liberalizing and protecting foreign investments, and does not recognize or attempt to deal with the negative aspects.

The draft Code recognized both the rights of the host countries and the right of TNCs to fair and equitable treatment.

The Code and the MAI are obviously the products of contrasting paradigms. The Code arose from the perception that the host developing countries, while having to accord some rights to TNCs, required an international understanding that TNCs have to comply with international guidelines that recognize the countries' development needs and national objectives, and that the hosts could by right allow the guest foreign investors to enter and operate on terms generally chosen by the hosts. The MAI, on the other hand, arose from the perceived need of foreign investors to expand and protect their interests from perceived interference by States that impose conditions on their operations. In this paradigm, the 'borderless world' is the ideal construct, and any barriers to the free flow of investments and to the right to investment, property ownership and unhindered operations must be considered 'distortions' and a denial of the investors' rights. The affirmation of these alleged investors' rights is seen as important to prevent States from constraining the expansionary reach and operations of foreign investors.

The aborted Code of Conduct on TNCs was the main set

of international guidelines that were to have dealt generally with the relations between TNCs or foreign investors and States. However, there are a number of other codes and guidelines that the UN system has established or attempted to establish that cover more specific issues.

These include the UNCTAD-based Set of Multilaterally Agreed Equitable Principles and Rules for the Control of Restrictive Business Practices (adopted in 1980 by the UN General Assembly) and the Draft International Code of Conduct on the Transfer of Technology (which has not yet been adopted by the General Assembly); the International Labour Organization (ILO) Tripartite Declaration of Principles Concerning Multinational Enterprises and Social Policy (1977); the World Health Organization (WHO)-based International Code of Marketing of Breast-Milk Substitutes (1981); and the Guidelines for Consumer Protection (based on a UN General Assembly resolution in 1985). In the environmental field, there are also international legal agreements (such as the Basel Convention banning the export of hazardous wastes to developing countries) that have an influence on the behaviour of international companies.

These instruments have the intention of influencing the behaviour of foreign investors and TNCs so that they conform to development needs or fulfil social and environmental obligations. Together they would also constitute elements of an alternative approach to an international policy or framework on foreign investment. Such a framework, encompassing the various existing instruments, could be further developed through additional instruments covering other areas by sector and issue.

The recent history of evolving an international framework for foreign investment shows that the proposed MAI (and models based on it) constitutes only one approach. It is an approach based on a paradigm that seeks to protect foreign investors' rights to the exclusion of their obligations and of host countries' rights. An alternative approach would take into account the rights and obligations of host countries and foreign investors, ensure that these are properly balanced, and be based on the primary objective of contributing to economic development and social and environmental objectives. It is, however, an issue for debate as to whether such an approach is possible in the present global environment, and also what would constitute an appropriate venue for discussions on the investment issue.

Proposals for appropriate management of foreign investment

Summary of conclusions

Previous sections have emphasized the following points:

(i) There are various categories of foreign investment, and it is important for governments to distinguish between the different types, understand the characteristics and effects of each type, and formulate policies to deal with each.

(ii) Even for the apparently most beneficial type, FDI, where there can be important contributions to the development of host countries, it is academically recognized that there are also potential costs and risks, among the most important of which are financial instability and balance-of-payments difficulties.

(iii) Therefore a policy framework for managing FDI must take into account the need to attempt to maximize the benefits while reducing the costs and risks.

(iv) Thus, governments, especially those of the developing countries, because of their greater vulnerability, need to be able to formulate policies that:

(a) distinguish the types of FDI that are appropriate;

(b) encourage the entry of FDI considered desirable, while discouraging or disallowing FDI considered not so appropriate to the country;

(c) impose certain conditions, if found necessary, on the operations of FDI; and

(d) subject FDI policy to wider national objectives and development needs.

(v) The MAI approach is too one-sided in its objectives and functions of protecting and furthering foreign investors' interests while denying the interests of host States and countries. Moreover, there is the assumption that there is no need to distinguish between different types of foreign investment, that all foreign investments bring only benefits but no costs, and the articles of the MAI were therefore drawn up under these assumptions. Social, cultural, development, environmental and human rights concerns are also ignored in this approach.

(vi) There have been other attempts at creating international frameworks dealing with foreign investments or the behaviour of foreign enterprises. Some of these have been more accommodating to the rights and needs of host developing countries and to the imperatives of development. It would be useful to revisit some of these attempts and to examine the usefulness of reviving, improving or extending them, as well as to examine new approaches.

Given the above conclusions, this section attempts to provide suggestions for elements of an appropriate approach or framework for the management of foreign investment. Proposals will be confined mainly to FDI. The proposals are categorized into national-level and international-level approaches and actions.

National-level policies and actions

SELECTIVE POLICY ON AND STRATEGIC APPROACH TO FDI

In view of empirical evidence on the benefits and costs of FDI, developing countries should have a selective policy and strategic approach towards FDI. The right of entry and establishment should thus be conferred by a State on chosen foreign investors, and not be taken as an inherent right of the investors. Historically, many presently developed countries and the more advanced developing countries had such a selective policy. For example, Japan and the Republic of Korea had very little FDI (in 1984–1994, FDI inflows to Japan were less than one-tenth of one per cent of gross domestic capital formation), and the Republic of Korea and Taiwan Province of China had important restrictions on FDI entry and degree of foreign ownership. Yet these countries are among the fastest growing in the world. China and Malaysia have allowed much more FDI but they also have a selective approach in terms of opening up certain sectors where foreign firms can contribute to technological and export development while discouraging FDI in other sectors where domestic companies either are weak (and need protection) or already possess technical capability (as in agriculture).

NEED TO DISTINGUISH BETWEEN THE DIFFERING CAPACITIES AND NEEDS OF LOCAL AND FOREIGN INVESTORS

An indiscriminate policy of opening up and of treating foreign firms on equal or better terms than local firms could lead to deindustrialization in a country where the local enterprises are too weak to compete on equal terms with foreign firms. Thus, developing countries should be allowed to continue to protect certain sectors or industries where there is considerable local investment (or where the State is encouraging attempts to build up local capacity).

In principle, State assistance to local enterprises should be looked at not as a 'distortion', or as necessarily wasteful or somehow unethical, but possibly as legitimate affirmative action to help the weak companies eventually to stand on their own. There are advantages to national development for local enterprise or farm development to occur, since institutions belonging to nationals are more likely to make use of local materials and talents, generate more domestic linkages, and retain profits locally for reinvestment, all of which are positive for economic growth and development.

Thus, a blanket 'national treatment' policy towards foreign

investment is inadvisable, as a 'level playing field' for local and foreign investors is likely to result in more unequal results when the capacities are unequal, as foreign investors are larger and will be starting from a much stronger position.

NEED TO ENSURE ACCEPTABLE TREATMENT OF INVESTORS

In order to obtain FDI that is considered beneficial for national development, developing countries have to establish conditions that are attractive to foreign firms. This may include guarantees for their unhindered operations, the exercise of expropriation only in extreme circumstances and even then with adequate compensation at rates that can in principle be worked out beforehand (so that the investor knows what the terms are), and freedom to remit profits generated from FDI. Other, and perhaps more important, conditions include political and social stability, security, good infrastructure, a credible legal system with due process, a trained or trainable labour force, tax and other incentives, etc. Each country should, however, be given the space to determine which elements it chooses to adopt and act on.

SOCIAL AND ENVIRONMENTAL SCREENING AND OBLIGATIONS OF FOREIGN INVESTORS

Although developing countries may exert great efforts to attract the investors they desire, their right to request that foreign investors fulfil certain obligations and thus follow some conditions should be recognized. These may include the transfer of technology; the training and employment of local workers, professionals and executives; the development of linkages to the domestic sectors; and providing local participation or partnership in equity ownership.

In light of a country's social and environmental goals and the need to maintain or raise standards, governments should carefully screen foreign investment applications and discourage or reject those projects or enterprises that would be socially or culturally detrimental (for example, those resulting in net loss of jobs, endangering health and safety of workers or consumers, promoting unsustainable consumption patterns and lifestyles or adversely affecting local cultural norms) or that would damage or pollute the environment (for example, through exploitation of natural resources that should be conserved or through use of harmful technology).

As part of the processes of application, selection and approval, foreign investments should undergo an environmental impact assessment and a social impact assessment. Only those that are positively assessed should be approved, and with conditions if necessary. Moreover, foreign investors may be asked not only to operate with respect for domestic laws, but also to contribute positively to social and environmental development.

ASSESSING THE EFFECTS ON THE LOCAL ECONOMY

In their FDI selection system, developing countries should include an assessment of the effects of the proposed investment on the local economy, especially local enterprises, farms and the informal sector. For example, positive criteria for projects under application could include that the projects do not compete with existing local enterprises or farms, and that they contribute new appropriate technologies and have significant linkages with the domestic economy; while adverse factors could include significant displacement of existing local firms accompanied by loss of jobs, heavy dependence on imported inputs with little demand for local resources or locally produced inputs, and substitution of existing appropriate local products with inappropriate new products (e.g., expensive, non-nutritious fast foods potentially replacing more nutritious local foods).

PROTECTING FINANCIAL STABILITY AND THE BALANCE OF PAYMENTS

Most importantly, in formulating their FDI policies, governments of developing countries should take into account the need to protect their economies from the risks of financial instability and of getting into balance-of-payments or foreign exchange difficulties. Thus, foreign investors and their proposed projects should be carefully assessed with regard to the possible effects their activities would have on the nation's financial stability, foreign exchange position and balance of payments.

International-level policies and actions

NEED FOR A FRESH LOOK AT THE NATURE AND EFFECTS OF FOREIGN INVESTMENTS

The nature and effects of cross-border foreign investments as a whole should be reviewed from an overall and balanced perspective. Just as the claims about the unalloyed positive effects of short-term capital have been brought down to earth by the Asian financial crisis, it is possible that events will in future also show that the positive aspects of FDI are matched by some negative effects.

It is thus important that a comprehensive review be made

of the nature and the positive and negative effects of all kinds
of foreign investment, and of the conditions for the successful
use and management of each. Such a comprehensive and
balanced approach is especially needed now as the global
financial crisis has left in its wake a desperate search for causes,
solutions and correct policies.

RECONSIDERATION OF AN APPROPRIATE INTERNATIONAL APPROACH TO
FOREIGN INVESTMENT AND INVESTORS' RIGHTS

Given the inadequacies of theory and policy shown up by the
financial and economic crises, it is timely for a reconsideration
of international approaches to international investment.
There should not be a continued 'rush forward' with international policies and especially legally binding agreements
that 'lock' the vulnerable developing countries into a process
of capital and investment liberalization under an MAI or MAI-
type model of international arrangements on investment.

The global financial and economic crisis, which is significantly related to cross-border capital flows, signifies a new
circumstance that calls for a deep study and reassessment of
recent trends in thinking on the nature of international capital
movements. The next few years therefore should be devoted
by the international community to an educative process on a
wide range of investment issues. Until such a study process
yields adequate insights to enable policy conclusions to be
drawn, there should not be initiatives to negotiate or promote
a legally binding international agreement furthering the rights
of foreign investors in areas such as their movement and establishment, national treatment and compensation. In particular,
there should not be any further initiatives for furthering inter-

national arrangements which constrict or deny the host States their right or capacity to determine both the role of foreign investment in their economy, and the conditions for the entry and establishment of foreign investment; nor their require-ment that foreign investors fulfil obligations towards the national development, social and environmental goals of host countries.

STRENGTHENING EXISTING INTERNATIONAL ARRANGEMENTS AND PROMOTING NEW ONES FOR CHANNELLING FOREIGN INVESTMENTS TOWARDS DEVELOPMENT, SOCIAL AND ENVIRONMENTAL GOALS

International arrangements for facilitating or ensuring the implementation of the positive social, developmental and environmental roles of foreign investments and investors should be strengthened. For example:

(i) the implementation of the Set of Multilaterally Agreed Equitable Principles and Rules for the Control of Re-strictive Business Practices (based in UNCTAD) should be strengthened, and the negotiations on the Draft In-ternational Code of Conduct on the Transfer of Tech-nology could be revived;

(ii) the WHO-based Code of Marketing of Breast-Milk Substitutes could serve as a model for similar guidelines relating to the marketing of other products;

(iii) the UN General Assembly's Guidelines for Consumer Protection should be strengthened and subjected to better monitoring and implementation;

(iv) in the context of the implementation of Agenda 21, the Commission on Sustainable Development could establish a process of obliging enterprises, especially those engaged in cross-border investments, to respect international standards on environmental issues;

(v) a new international effort can be initiated to facilitate a process or an arrangement whereby foreign investors are required to respect and contribute to the development, social and environmental objectives, policies and practices of host countries; this could incorporate some elements from the draft Code of Conduct on TNCs;

(vi) the process of establishing new protocols and conventions to protect the environment should be accelerated while the existing agreements should be strengthened, in view of the increasing global crisis of the environment. These agreements should specifically include provisions on criteria for good practices of and policies on foreign investments and the role and responsibilities of foreign investors.

CHAPTER 5

GENERAL CONCLUSIONS AND PROPOSALS

Balancing opportunities and problems resulting from globalization

Among the biggest dilemmas for developing countries is whether they should open themselves up to the globalization process (in the hope of obtaining some of the benefits) or take a more cautious approach to avoid risks (which would attract criticisms from the mainstream institutions that are sure to lecture the countries concerned that they will be left behind).

The challenge is whether developing countries can take advantage of the liberalization process, which to a large extent is being pushed on them externally, while at the same time avoiding or minimizing the disruptive consequences on their societies and economies. The ability to manage liberalization and globalization will be a crucial aspect of national policy-making in the years ahead. At this point the danger is that most developing countries, under great pressure from agencies such as the WTO, the IMF and the World Bank, will go along with the trend and institute more, as well as rapid, liberalization policies, without a clear idea of the conditions needed to address the associated risks successfully.

Instead of rapid liberalization, a selective approach to liberalization is more appropriate. The aim of this would be to strike a careful balance between opening the domestic market (to benefit consumers) and protecting it (to take into account the interests of small producers especially).

A useful summary of the opportunities and challenges of globalization has been given in the UNCTAD Secretary-General's report to the ninth session of the Conference (UNCTAD, 1996a). The main opportunities it lists are: trading opportunities arising from the Uruguay Round; opportunities from international capital flows and financing of development (UNCTAD warned of the risks involved as well, and noted that the majority of developing countries did not enjoy these facilities); opportunities provided by international production through FDI; and increased opportunities for economic cooperation among developing countries (ECDC) to boost South–South cooperation.

The UNCTAD report also warns of the risks, stating that 'the processes of globalization and liberalization can also give rise to a number of potential negative consequences and challenges to development'. It gives details of the following three problems: loss of policy autonomy (the range of policy instruments available to developing countries has narrowed as a result of economic liberalization policies and stringent multilateral disciplines); financial openness and the risk of instability and disruption to development sentiments of external investors; and the phenomenon of marginalization (in which some developing countries, especially LDCs, are unable to benefit from or participate meaningfully in globalization due to structural supply-side weaknesses and debt).

Although the UNCTAD report provides a useful summary of some important implications of globalization, it is by no means exhaustive. The summary does, however, point to the immense difficulties that face many (perhaps most) developing countries in their trying to survive or thrive in a globalized economy. The LDCs have too many problems such as debt and low commodity prices, and too weak an infrastructure and capacity, to develop industrial exports. At the same time they face the threat of local firms and farms being overrun by foreign products and companies as their countries liberalize. Even the stronger developing countries find great difficulties in being able to manage and balance the costs and benefits of globalization, as the recent financial crisis in East Asian countries has shown.

The need for South–South policy coordination among developing countries

In order to widen their policy options in the future and to strengthen their bargaining power, developing countries have to organize themselves to strive for a more democratic global system.

Countries of the South, at many different forums, have collectively reaffirmed their view that the social and economic role of the UN and its agencies is even more necessary in view of globalization. While they may have spoken up, they have to do even more to assert their belief in the UN's role and to intensify the fight to reverse its decline. They should also strengthen South–South cooperation, with the support of UN agencies such as UNCTAD and UNDP as well as through their own mechanisms and organizations. This cooperation should include an increase in trade, investment and communications links at the bilateral level and between regions, as well as joint projects involving several South countries.

Equally or even more urgently required is South–South cooperation in the area of policy coordination in reaching common positions. This is especially because policies that used to be taken at the national level as the prerogative of national governments are increasingly being made at forums, institutions and negotiations at both the international and regional levels. Without a more effective collective voice at such international forums, Southern countries will find even more that their national policies on economic, social and cultural matters will be made and dominated by the more powerful Northern governments and the institutions they control.

At present there are few institutions of the South and their capacity is weak. Like-minded countries of the South should consider initiatives to start or strengthen centres of research and coordination, including those that are independent or private, that can help them in their preparations for negotiations as well as strategic thinking and long-term planning. Greater collaboration among regional institutions of the South (for example, ASEAN, SAARC, SADC, Mercosur, Caricom, etc.), especially in sharing of information and coordination of policies and positions, would be beneficial.

Among the objectives of South–South policy coordination could be efforts to strengthen the UN system and to democratize international institutions and relations, which are covered below.

The need for appropriate and democratic global governance

In order for developing countries to avoid bleak prospects in the 21st century, they must be given the space and opportunity to strengthen their economies and to develop their social infrastructure, while having environmentally sound practices. For this to happen, there has to be a much more favourable international environment, starting with the democratization of international relations and institutions, so that the South can have an active role in decision-making.

The developing countries should have more rights of participation in decision-making processes in the IMF, World Bank and WTO, which should also be made more accountable to the public and to local and poor communities. These institutions have been under the control of the governments of developed countries due to the systems of decision-making and governance. There has long been a perception that as a result of such dominance, the three institutions have tended to have policies or rules that are biased towards the interests of the developed countries, while developing countries have either benefited less or suffered from the wrong policies and biased rules. There is thus a need to reform the decision-making processes so as to give developing countries their right to adequate participation; and to review and, where needed, to change the content of policies and rules so that they reflect the interests of developing countries that form the majority of the membership.

As it is the most universal and democratic international forum, the UN and its agencies should be given the opportunity and resources to maintain their identity, have their approach and development focus reaffirmed, and strengthen their programmes and activities. The strong trend of removing the resources and authority of the UN in global economic and social issues, in favour of the Bretton Woods institutions and the WTO, should be reversed.

In particular, those Northern countries that have downgraded their commitment to the UN should reverse this attitude and, instead, affirm its indispensable and valuable role in advocating the social and developmental dimension in the process of rapid global change. The world, especially the developing countries, require that this dimension be kept alive and indeed strengthened greatly; otherwise there is a danger that a monolithic *laissez-faire* approach to globalization and to development will cause immense harm.

Only a great strengthening of the UN will allow it to play its compensatory role more significantly and effectively. But of course a complementary 'safety net' function is the minimum that should be set for the UN. For the South as well as the international community to make progress towards redressing the basic inequities in the international system, the UN must be able to make the leap from merely offsetting the social fallout of unequal structures and liberalization, to fighting against the basic causes of poverty, inequities, social tensions and unsustainable development. The more this is done, the more options and chances there will be for developing countries in future.

It is vital that the UN continues to promote developing countries' rights and interests, an equitable world order and the realization of human and development rights as its central economic and social goals. There is a danger that some UN agencies (and the Secretariat itself) may be influenced by conservative political forces to join in the *laissez-faire* approach or merely be content to play a second-fiddle role of taking care of the adverse social effects of *laissez-faire* policies promoted by other agencies. The UN should therefore keep true to its mission of promoting appropriate development and justice for the world's people, and always advocate for policies and programmes that promote this mission; otherwise it too will lose its credibility.

Rebalancing the roles of State and market

In considering their options in the globalized economy, developing countries have to review seriously the liberalization experience and make important conclusions on the balance and mix between the roles of the State and the market. As the Indian economists Amit Bhaduri and Deepak Nayyar (1996) have argued, contrary to the *laissez-faire* structural adjustment model, both the market and the State have key roles. According to them, an unbridled economic role for the government in the name of distributive justice is often a recipe for disaster in the long run, but, on the other hand, market solutions are often ruthless to the poor. Moreover, government failure does not imply that a reliance only on markets will succeed.

The study warns against fundamentalism in belief in either State or market. While there are failures in State policies, there can also be serious market failures. What is important is to recognize both government and market failures and

introduce correcting devices against both. The proper func-
tioning of a market needs the support and guidance of the
State, while conversely the State cannot do without the
markets. Looking at the experience of the late industrializers,
the authors conclude that the belief that markets know best,
or that State intervention is counterproductive in the process
of industrialization, is not borne out by their history.

Experience from the second half of the 20th century
suggests that the guiding and supportive role of the State has
been the very foundation of successful development in
countries which are latecomers to industrialization. State
intervention created the initial conditions for industrialization
through State investment in infrastructure, development of
human resources and agrarian reform. In the early stages of
industrialization, a key role of the State was protection of infant
industries through tariffs and other means. In the later stages of
industrialization, the nature of State intervention in the
market must change and become functional, institutional or
strategic.

The search for
appropriate development strategies

The review of structural adjustment policies, and of the liberal
'free-market' model in general, shows that a reconceptualiza-
tion of development strategies is required and that alternative
approaches are needed.

An important issue is whether developing countries will
be allowed to learn lessons from and adopt key aspects of
these alternative approaches. For this to happen, the policy

conditions imposed through structural adjustment have to be loosened, and some of the multilateral disciplines exerted on developing countries through the WTO agreements have to be reexamined.

In the search for alternative options for developing countries, work also has to be increased on developing economic and development approaches that are based on the principles of sustainable development. The integration of environmental and economic concerns, and in a socially equitable manner, is perhaps the most important challenge for developing countries and for the world as a whole in the next few decades.

However, international discussions on the environment can only reach a satisfactory conclusion if they are conducted within an agreed equitable framework. The North, with its indisputable power, should not make the environmental issue a new instrument of domination over the South. It should be accepted by all that the North should carry the bulk of the burden and responsibility for adjustment towards more ecologically sound forms of production. This is because most of the present global environmental problems are due mainly to the North, which also possesses the financial resources and the economic capacity to reduce their output and consumption levels.

In the 21st century, much more focus has to be placed on changing economic policies and behaviour in order that the patterns of consumption and production can be made environmentally sound. What needs to be discussed is not only the development model of the South but much more the economic model of the North and of course the international economic order.

There is also a need to strive for governance at a national level that combines economic development, environmental concerns and social justice. In both North and South, the wide disparities in wealth and income within countries have to be narrowed. In a situation of improved equity, it would be more possible to plan and implement strategies of economic adjustment to ecological and social goals.

REFERENCES

AKYÜZ Y (1995). Taming international finance. In: Michie J and Grieve-smith J, eds. *Managing the Global Economy*. Oxford, Oxford University Press.

AKYÜZ Y (2000). Causes and sources of the Asian financial crisis. Paper presented at Host Country Event at UNCTAD X, Bangkok, February.

BHADURI A and NAYYAR D (1996). *The Intelligent Person's Guide to Liberalization*. New Delhi, Penguin Books.

CLAIRMONT F F (1996). *The Rise and Fall of Economic Liberalism: The Making of the Economic Gulag*. Penang, Malaysia, Southbound and Third World Network.

DAS B L (1998). *The WTO Agreements: Deficiencies, Imbalances and Required Changes*. Penang, Malaysia, Third World Network.

DAS B L (1999). *Some Suggestions for Improvements in the WTO Agreements*. Penang, Malaysia, Third World Network.

EUROPEAN COMMISSION (1995). A level playing field for FDI worldwide. Briefing Paper. Brussels.

FAO (1999). Experience with the implementation of the Uruguay Round agreement on agriculture, synthesis of country case studies (mimeo). Rome, Food and Agriculture Organization of the United Nations, Commodities and Trade Division.

GHAZALI bin Atan (1990). An empirical evaluation of the effects of foreign capital inflows on the economy of Malaysia (1961–1986). PhD thesis. Kuala Lumpur, Faculty of Economics and Social Studies, International Development Centre.

GHAZALI bin Atan (1996). *The Effects of DFI on Trade, Balance of Payments and Growth in Developing Countries, and Appropriate Policy Approaches to*

DFI. Penang, Malaysia, Third World Network.

KHOR M (1993). *South–North Resource Flows*. Penang, Malaysia, Third World Network.

KHOR M (1998). *The Economic Crisis in East Asia: Causes, Effects, Lessons*. Penang, Malaysia, Third World Network.

KHOR M (1999). Foreign investment policy, the multilateral agreement on investment and development issues. Paper contributed to the *UNDP Human Development Report 1999*. New York, United Nations.

KOZUL–WRIGHT R and ROWTHORN R (1998). *Transnational Corporations and the Global Economy*. London, Macmillan.

KREGEL J A (1996). Some risks and implications of financial globalization for national autonomy. *UNCTAD Review, 1996*. New York and Geneva, United Nations.

NAYYAR D (1997). *Globalization: The Past in our Future*. Penang, Malaysia, Third World Network.

RAGHAVAN C (1990). *Recolonization: The Uruguay Round, GATT and the South*. Penang, Malaysia, Third World Network.

RICUPERO R (2000). From the Washington Consensus to the Bangkok Convergence. Secretary-General's closing speech at UNCTAD X, Bangkok, February.

RODRIK D (1999). *The New Global Economy and Developing Countries: Making Openness Work*. Washington DC, Overseas Development Council.

SHAFAEDDIN S M (1994). The impact of trade liberalization on export and GDP growth in least developed countries. *Discussion Paper No. 85*. Geneva, UNCTAD.

SOUTH CENTRE (1997). *Foreign Direct Investment, Development and the New Global Economic Order*. Geneva.

UNCTAD (1996a). *Globalization and Liberalization*. Report of the Secretary-General of UNCTAD to the ninth session of the Conference (TD/366/Rev.1). New York and Geneva, United Nations.

UNCTAD (1996b). *International Investment Instruments: A Compendium*. New York and Geneva, United Nations.

UNCTAD (1997). *Trade and Development Report, 1997*. New York and Geneva, United Nations.

UNCTAD (1998). *Trade and Development Report, 1998*. New York and

Geneva, United Nations.

UNCTAD (1999a). *Trade and Development Report, 1999*. New York and Geneva, United Nations.

UNCTAD (1999b). Industrial countries must work harder for development if globalization is to deliver on its promises. Press release (UNCTAD/INF/2816). 1 September.

UNCTAD (2000). *Report of the Secretary-General of UNCTAD to UNCTAD X* (TD/380). Geneva, February.

UNCTC (1990). The New Code environment. *UNCTC Current Studies Series A, No. 16*. New York, United Nations.

UNDP (1992). *Human Development Report 1992*. New York, United Nations.

UNDP (1999). *Human Development Report 1999*. New York, United Nations.

RECOMMENDED
FURTHER READING

Some readers may wish to go a little further into some of the key topics discussed in this book. We suggest here a handful of recommended titles which provide clear and illuminating explanations of some of the fundamental issues at stake, including a criticism of current arrangements and dominant beliefs, and some alternatives.

Debt
Peter Warburton, *Debt and Delusion*

Development and Globalization
Oscar Ugarteche, *The False Dilemma: Globalization – Opportunity or Threat?*

Foreign Direct Investment (FDI)
Martin Khor, *The Multilateral Agreement on Investment (UNDP)*
David Woodward, *The Next Crisis? Direct and Equity Investment in Developing Countries*

Free Trade
Graham Dunkley, *The Free Trade Adventure: the WTO, the Uruguay Round and Globalism: A Critique*
John Madeley, *Hungry for Trade: How the Poor Pay for Free Trade*

Global Financial System and its Reform

Walden Bello, Nicola Bullard and Kamal Malhotra (eds), *Global Finance: New Thinking on Regulating Speculative Capital Markets*

John Eatwell and Lance Taylor, *Global Finance at Risk*

Kavaljit Singh, *The Globalization of Finance: A Citizen's Guide*

Kavaljit Singh, *Taming Global Financial Flows: Challenges and Alternatives in the Era of Financial Globalization*

Neoliberal Economics

Amit Bhaduri and Deepak Nayyar, *The Intelligent Person's Guide to Liberalization*

Arthur MacEwan, *Neoliberalism or Democracy? Economic Strategy, Markets, and Alternatives for the 21st Century*

World Trade Organization (WTO)

B. L. Das, *An Introduction to the WTO Agreements*

B. L. Das, *The WTO Agreements: Deficiencies, Imbalances and Required Changes*

Chakravarti Raghavan, *Recolonization: GATT, the Uruguay Round and a New Global Economy*

RECOMMENDED
ORGANIZATIONS and WEBSITES

For further up-to-date information and analysis of the issues
dealt with in this book, readers will find the following
organizations and websites a useful starting point.

Focus on the Global South • www.focusweb.org
Group of 77 • www.g77.org
Institute for Agriculture and Trade Policy • www.iatp.org
Inter Press Service • www.ips.org
International Coalition for Development Action (ICDA)
 • www.icda.be
International Forum on Globalization • www.ifg.org
New Internationalist • www.newint.org
Social Watch • www.socialwatch.org
South Centre, Geneva • www.southcentre.org
Suns on line • www.sunsonline.org
Third World Network • www.twnside.org.sg
Third World Network, Latin American secretariat
 • www.redtercermundo.org.uy
United Nations Conference on Trade and Development
 (UNCTAD) • www.unctad.org
United Nations Development Programme (UNDP)
 • www.undp.org
United Nations Development Fund for Women (UNIFEM)
 • www.undp.org/unifem/
World Development Movement • www.wdm.org.uk

INDEX

The Global Issues Series

NOW AVAILABLE

Robert Ali Brac de la Perrière and Franck Seuret, *Brave New Seeds: The Threat of GM Crops to Farmers*

Oswaldo de Rivero, *The Myth of Development: The Non-viable Economies of the 21st Century*

Nicholas Guyatt, *Another American Century? The United States and the World after 2000*

Martin Khor, *Rethinking Globalization: Critical Issues and Policy Choices*

John Madeley, *Hungry for Trade: How the Poor Pay for Free Trade*

Riccardo Petrella, *The Water Manifesto: Arguments for a World Water Contract*

IN PREPARATION

Peggy Antrobus and Gigi Francisco, *The Women's Movement Worldwide: Issues and Strategies for the New Century*

Amit Bhaduri and Deepak Nayyar, *Free Market Economics: The Intelligent Person's Guide to Liberalization*

Julian Burger, *Indigenous Peoples: The Struggle of the World's Indigenous Nations and Communities*

Graham Dunkley, *Trading Development: Trade, Globalization and Alternative Development Possibilities*

Joyeeta Gupta, *Our Simmering Planet: What to do about Global Warming?*

John Howe, *A Ticket to Ride: Breaking the Transport Gridlock*

Susan Hawley, *Corruption: Privatization, Multinational Corporations and the Export of Bribery*

Calestous Juma, *The New Genetic Divide: Biotechnology in the Age of Globalization*

John Madeley, *The New Agriculture: Towards Food for All*

Jeremy Seabrook, *The Future of Culture: Can Human Diversity Survive in a Globalized World?*

Harry Shutt, *A New Globalism: Alternatives to the Breakdown of World Order*

David Sogge, *Give and Take: Foreign Aid in the New Century*

Keith Suter, *Curbing Corporate Power: How Can We Control Transnational Corporations?*

Oscar Ugarteche, *A Level Playing Field: Changing the Rules of the Global Economy*

Nedd Willard, *The Drugs War: Is This the Solution?*

For full details of this list and Zed's other subject and general catalogues, please write to: The Marketing Department, Zed Books, 7 Cynthia Street, London N1 9JF, UK
or email Sales@zedbooks.demon.co.uk

Visit our website at: http://www.zedbooks.demon.co.uk

PARTICIPATING ORGANIZATIONS

• **Both ENDS**
A service and advocacy organization which collaborates with
environment and indigenous organizations, both in the South and
in the North, with the aim of helping to create and sustain a
vigilant and effective environmental movement.

Damrak 28–30, 1012 LJ Amsterdam, The Netherlands
Phone: +31 20 623 08 23   Fax: +31 20 620 80 49
Email: info@bothends.org
Website: www.bothends.org

• **Catholic Institute for International Relations (CIIR)**
 CIIR aims to contribute to the eradication of poverty through a
programme that combines advocacy at national and international
level with community-based development.

Unit 3 Canonbury Yard, 190a New North Road, London N1 7BJ, UK
Phone: +44 (0) 20 7354 0883   Fax: +44 (0) 20 7359 0017
Email: ciir@ciir.org
Website: www.ciir.org

• **Corner House**
The Corner House is a UK-based research and solidarity group

working on social and environmental justice issues in North and South.

PO Box 3137, Station Road, Sturminster Newton, Dorset
DT10 1YJ, UK
Tel: +44 (0)1258 473795   Fax: +44 (0)1258 473748
Email cornerhouse@gn.apc.org
Website: www.cornerhouse.icaap.org

• **Council on International and Public Affairs (CIPA)**
CIPA is a human rights research, education and advocacy group, with a particular focus on economic and social rights in the USA and elsewhere around the world. Emphasis in recent years has been given to resistance to corporate domination.

777 United Nations Plaza, Suite 3C, New York, NY 10017, USA.
Tel: 212 972 9877   Fax: 212 972 9878
E-mail: cipany@igc.org
Website: www.cipa-apex.org

• **Dag Hammarskjöld Foundation**
The Dag Hammarskjöld Foundation, established 1962, organizes seminars and workshops on social, economic and cultural issues facing developing countries with a particular focus on alternative and innovative solutions. Results are published in its journal Develpment Dialogue.

Övre Slottsgatan 2, 753 10 Uppsala, Sweden
Tel: 46 18 102772   Fax: 46 18 122072
Email: secretariat@dhf.uu.se
web site: www.dhf.uu.se

- **Development GAP**

The Development Group for Alternative Policies is a Non-Profit Development Resource Organization working with popular organizations in the South and their Northern partners in support of a development that is truly sustainable and that advances social justice.

927 15th Street, NW – 4th Floor
Washington, DC 20005 - USA
Tel: + 1-202-898-1566   Fax: +1 202-898-1612
Email: dgap@igc.org
Website: www.developmentgap.org

- **Focus on the Global South**

Focus is dedicated to regional and global policy analysis and advocacy work. It works to strengthen the capacity of organizations of the poor and marginalized people of the South and to better analyse and understand the impacts of the globalization process on their daily lives.

c/o CUSRI, Chulalongkorn University, Bangkok 10330, Thailand
Tel: + 66 2 218 7363 Fax: + 66 2 255 9976
Email: Admin@focusweb.org
Website: www.focusweb.org

- **Inter Pares**

Inter Pares, a Canadian social justice organization, has been active since 1975 in building relationships with Third World development groups and providing support for community-based development programs. Inter Pares is also involved in education and advocacy in Canada, promoting understanding about the causes and effects of and solutions to, poverty.

58 rue Arthur Street, Ottawa, Ontario, K1R 7B9 Canada
Phone : + 1 (613) 563-4801   Fax: + 1 (613) 594-4704

- **Third World Network**

TWN is an international network of groups and individuals
involved in efforts to bring about a greater articulation of the needs
and rights of peoples in the Third World; a fair distribution of the
world's resources; and forms of development which are
ecologically sustainable and fulfil human needs. Its international
secretariat is based in Penang, Malaysia.

228 Macalister Road, 10400 Penang, Malaysia
Tel: +60-4-2266159   Fax: +60-4-2264505
Email: twnet@po.jaring.my   Website: www.twnside.org.sg

- **Third World Network–Africa**

TWN–Africa is engaged in research and advocacy on economic,
environmental and gender issues. In relation to its current particular interest in globalization and Africa, its work focuses on trade and
investment, the extractive sectors and gender and economic reform.

2 Ollenu Street, East Legon, P O Box AN19452, Accra-North, Ghana.
Tel: + 233 21 511189/503669/500419   Fax: + 233 21 51188
E-mail: twnafrica@ghana.com

- **World Development Movement (WDM)**

The World Development Movement campaigns to tackle the
causes of poverty and injustice. It is a democratic membership
movement that works with partners in the South to cancel
unpayable debt and break the ties of IMF conditionality, for fairer
trade and investment rules, and for strong international rules on
multinationals.

25 Beehive Place, London SW9 7QR, UK
Tel: +44 20 7737 6215   Fax: +44 20 7274 8232
E-mail: wdm@wdm.org.uk
Website: www.wdm.org.uk

THIS BOOK IS AVAILABLE IN THE FOLLOWING COUNTRIES

FIJI
University Book Centre
University of South Pacific
Suva

Tel: 679 313 900
Fax: 679 303 265

GHANA
EPP Book Services
P O Box TF 490
Trade Fair
Accra

Tel: 233 21 773087
Fax: 233 21 779099

MALAYSIA
Third World Network
228 Macalister Road
10400 Penang

Tel: 60 4 229 3511
Fax: 60 4 229 8106

MOZAMBIQUE
Sul Sensacoes
PO Box 2242,
Maputo

Tel: 258 1 421974
Fax: 258 1 423414

NEPAL
Everest Media Services
GPO Box 5443, Dillibazar
Putalisadak Chowk
Kathmandu

Tel: 977 1 416026
Fax: 977 1 250176

PAPUA NEW GUINEA
Unisearch PNG Pty Ltd
Box 320, University
National Capital District

Tel: 675 326 0130
Fax: 675 326 0127

RWANDA
Librairie Ikirezi
PO Box 443, Kigali

Tel/Fax: 250 71314

TANZANIA
TEMA Publishing Co Ltd
PO Box 63115
Dar Es Salaam

Tel: 255 51 113608
Fax: 255 51 110472

UGANDA
Aristoc Booklex Ltd
PO Box 5130, Kampala Road
Diamond Trust Building
Kampala

Tel/Fax: 256 41 254867

ZAMBIA
UNZA Press
PO Box 32379
Lusaka

Tel: 260 1 290409
Fax: 260 1 253952

ZIMBABWE
Weaver Press
P O Box A1922
Avondale, Harare

Tel: 263 4 308330
Fax: 263 4 339645